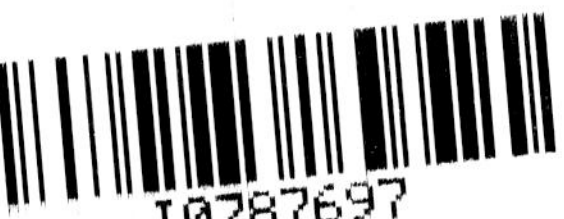

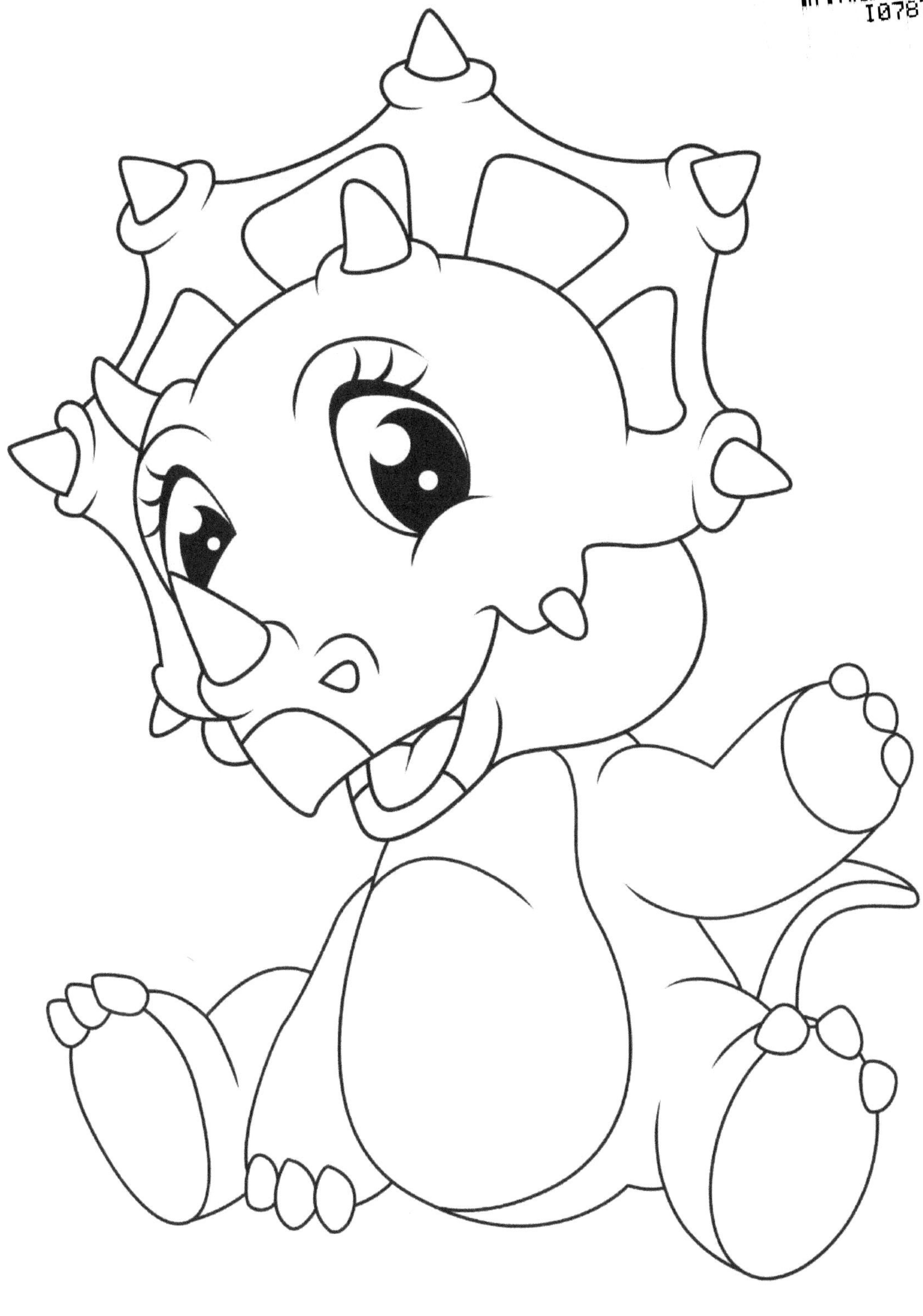

This book belongs to :

....

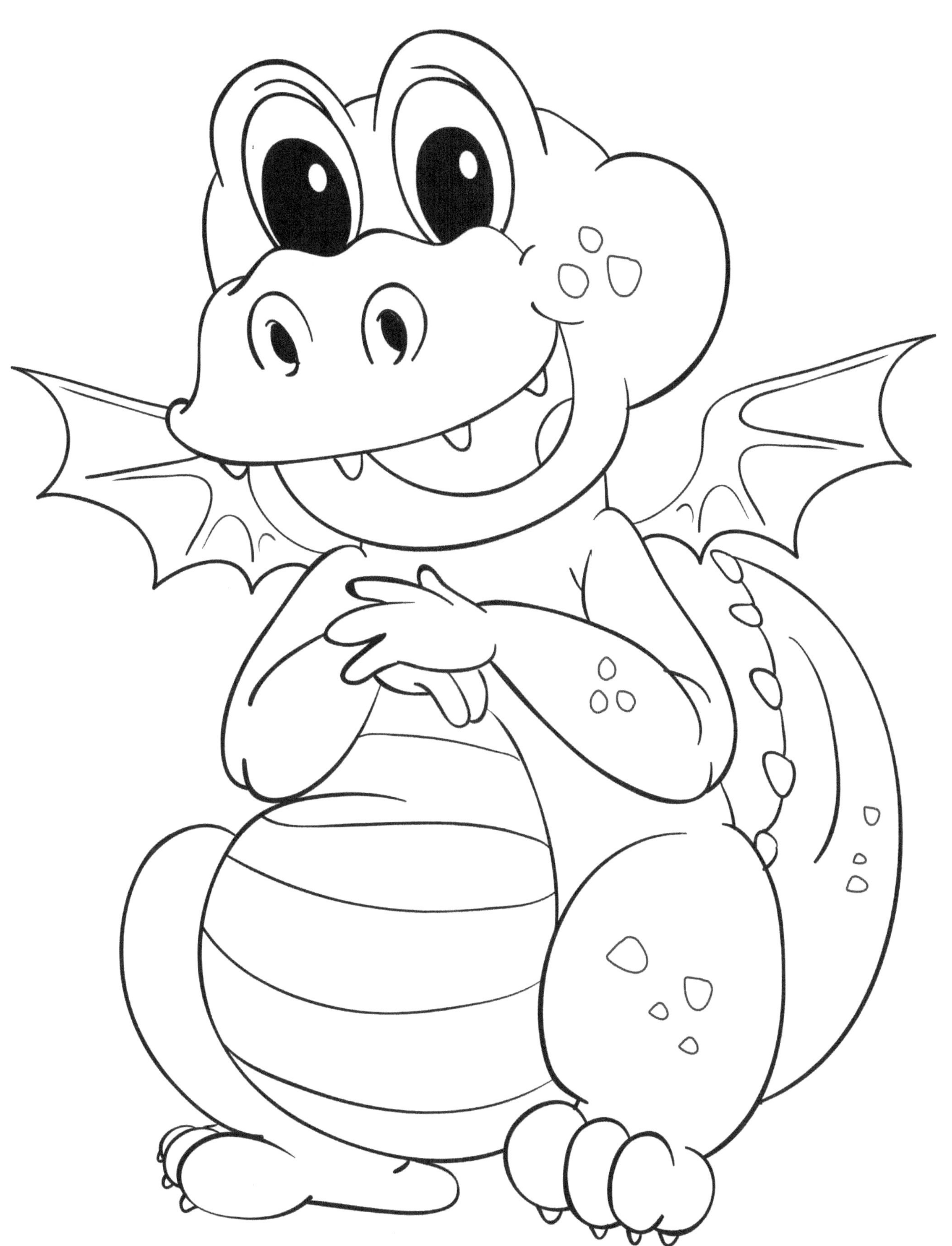

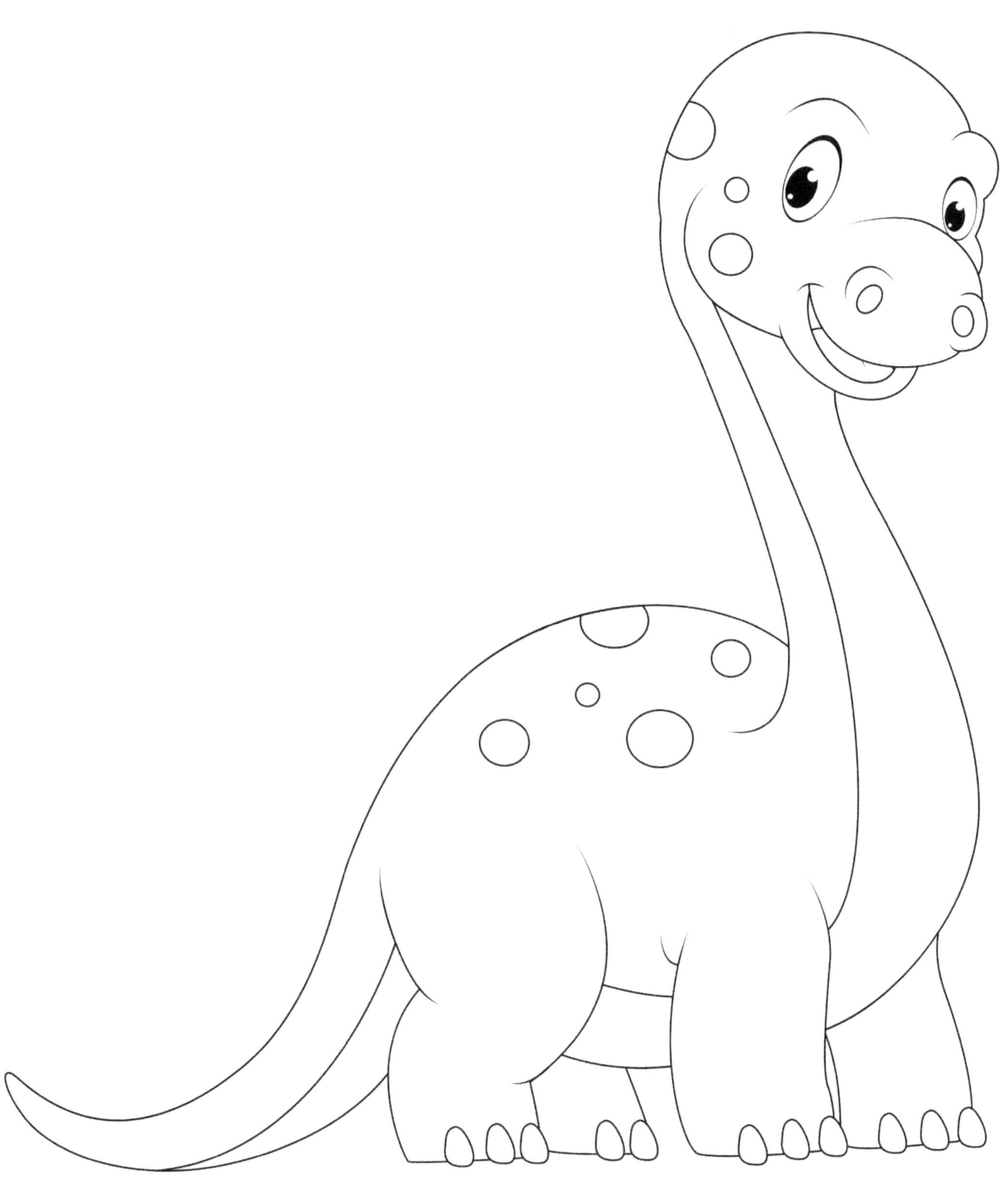

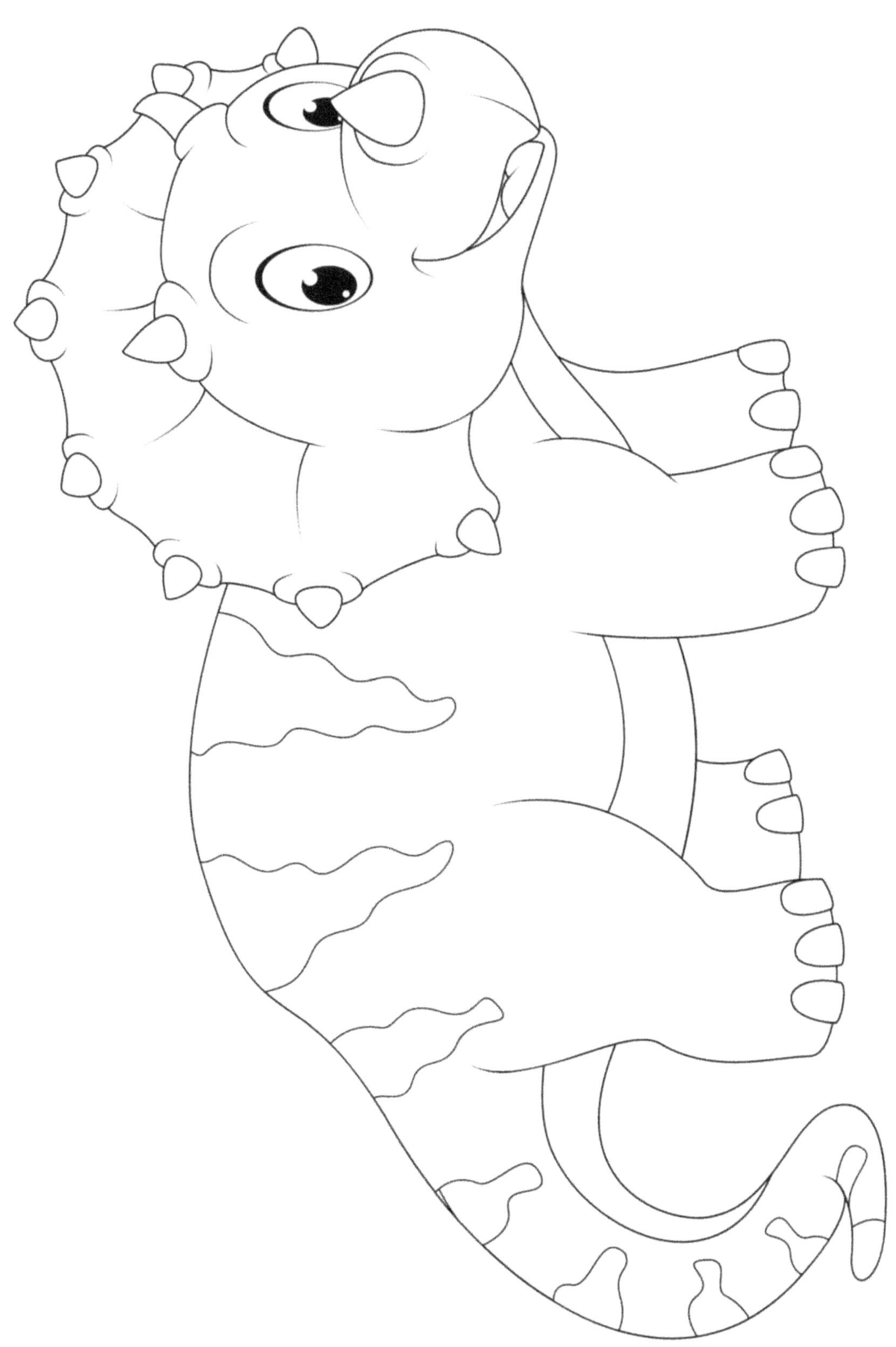

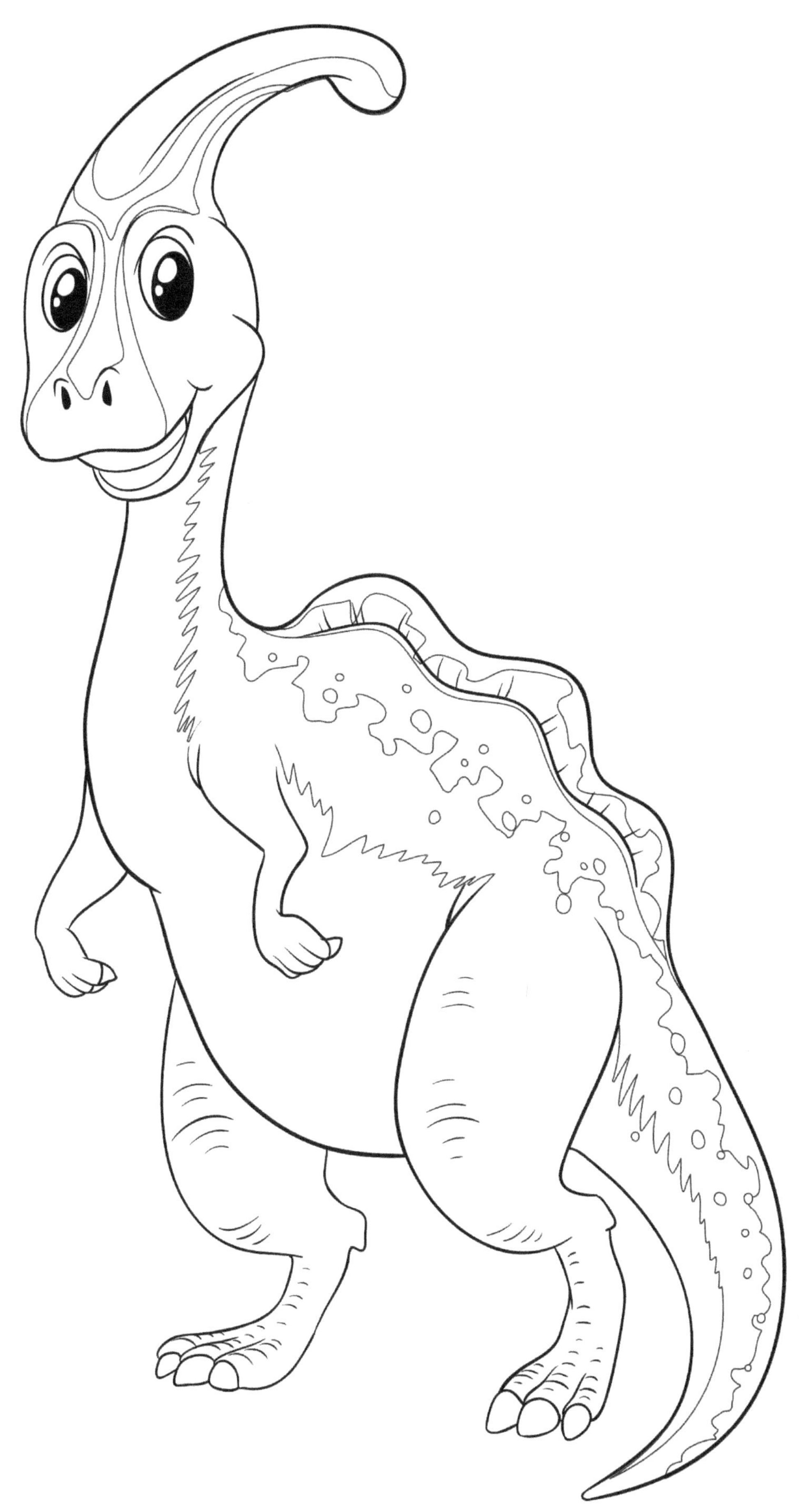

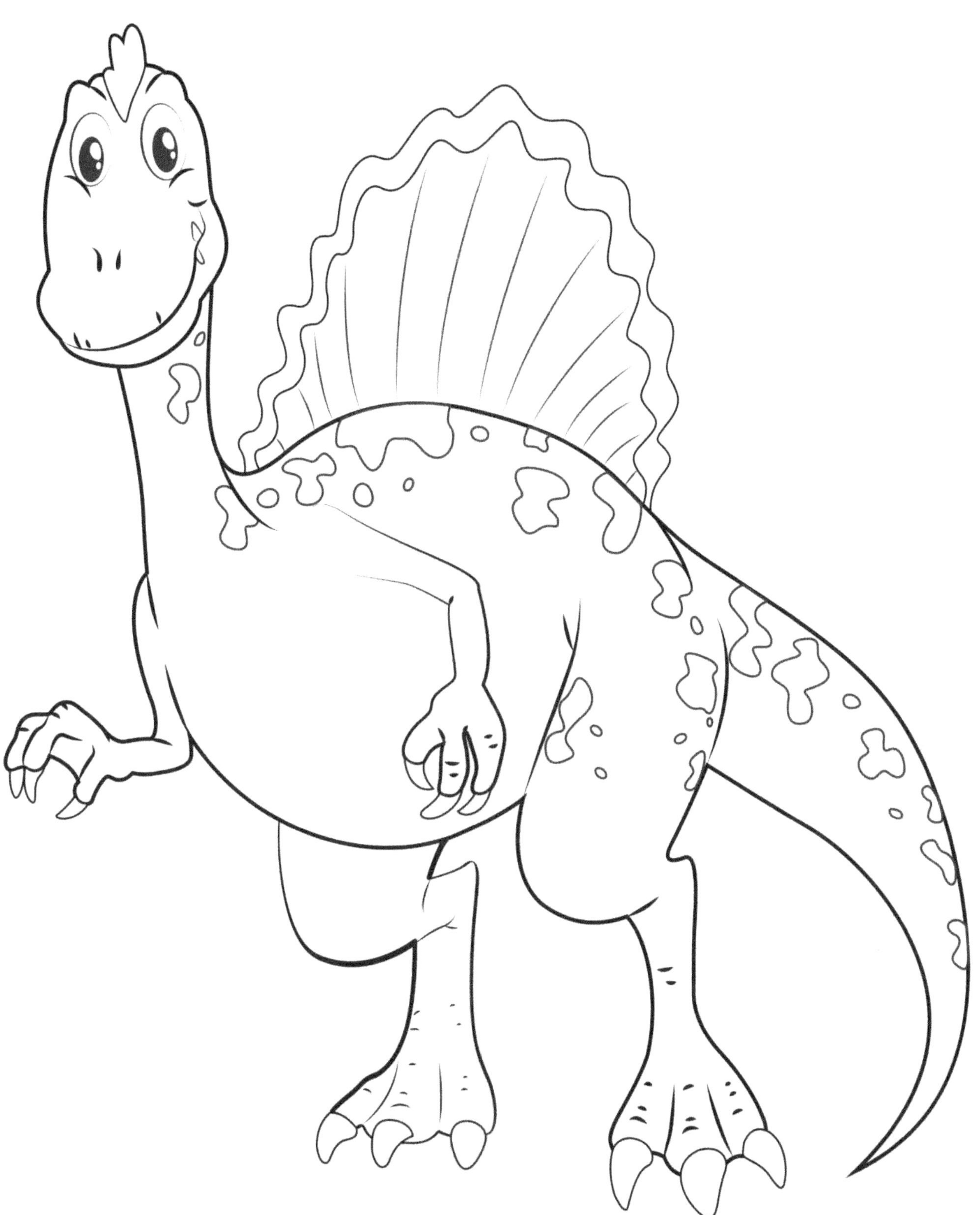

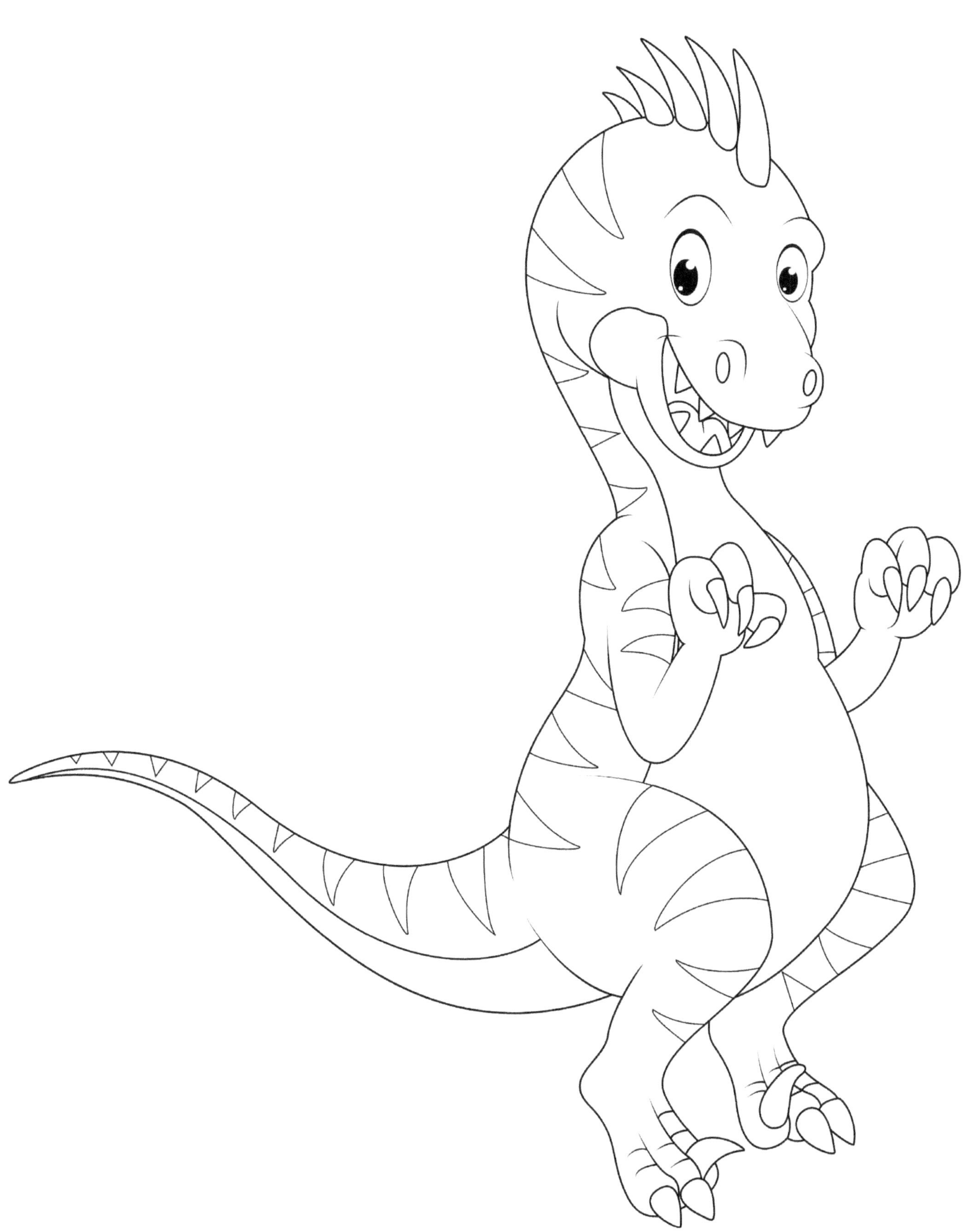

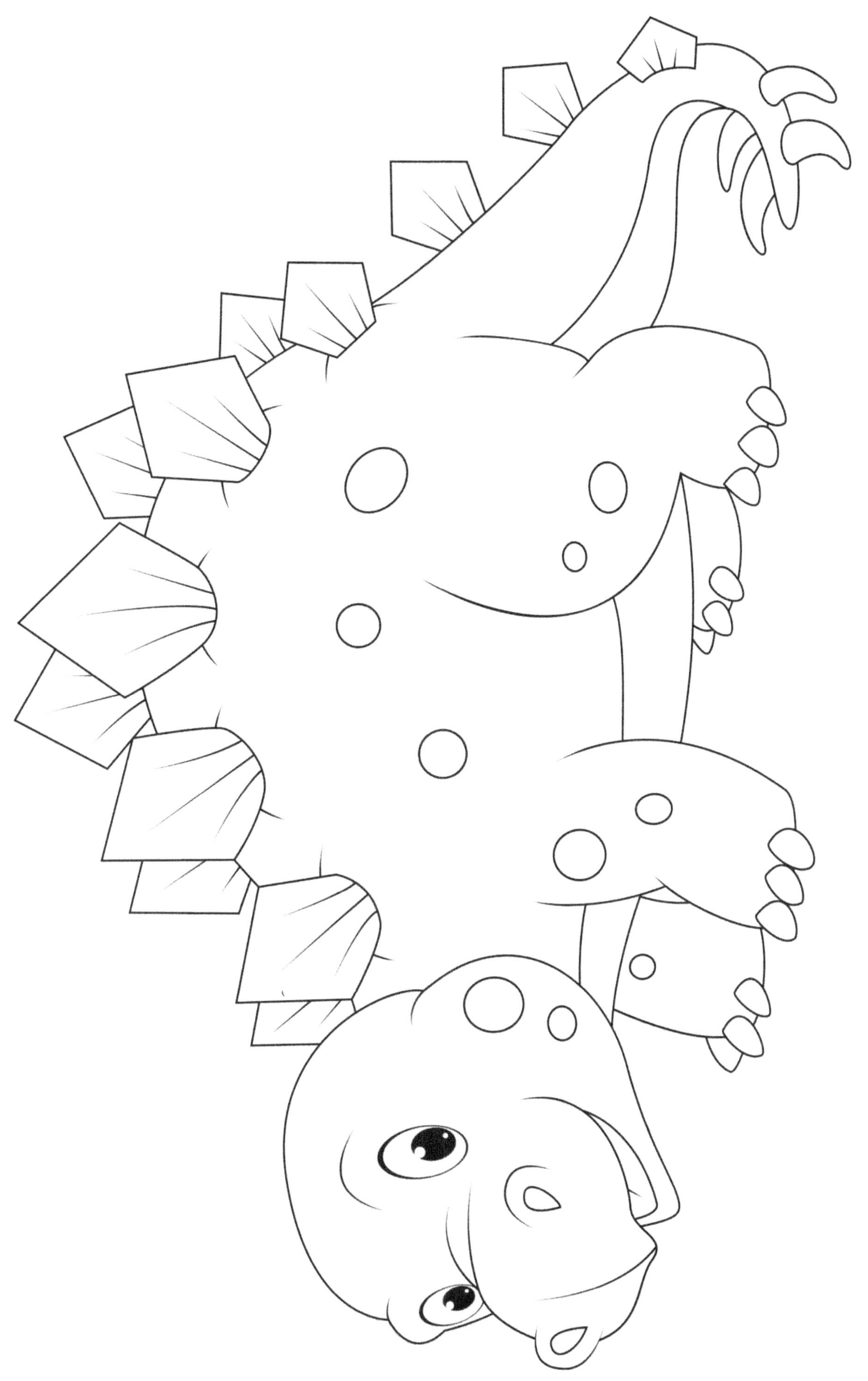

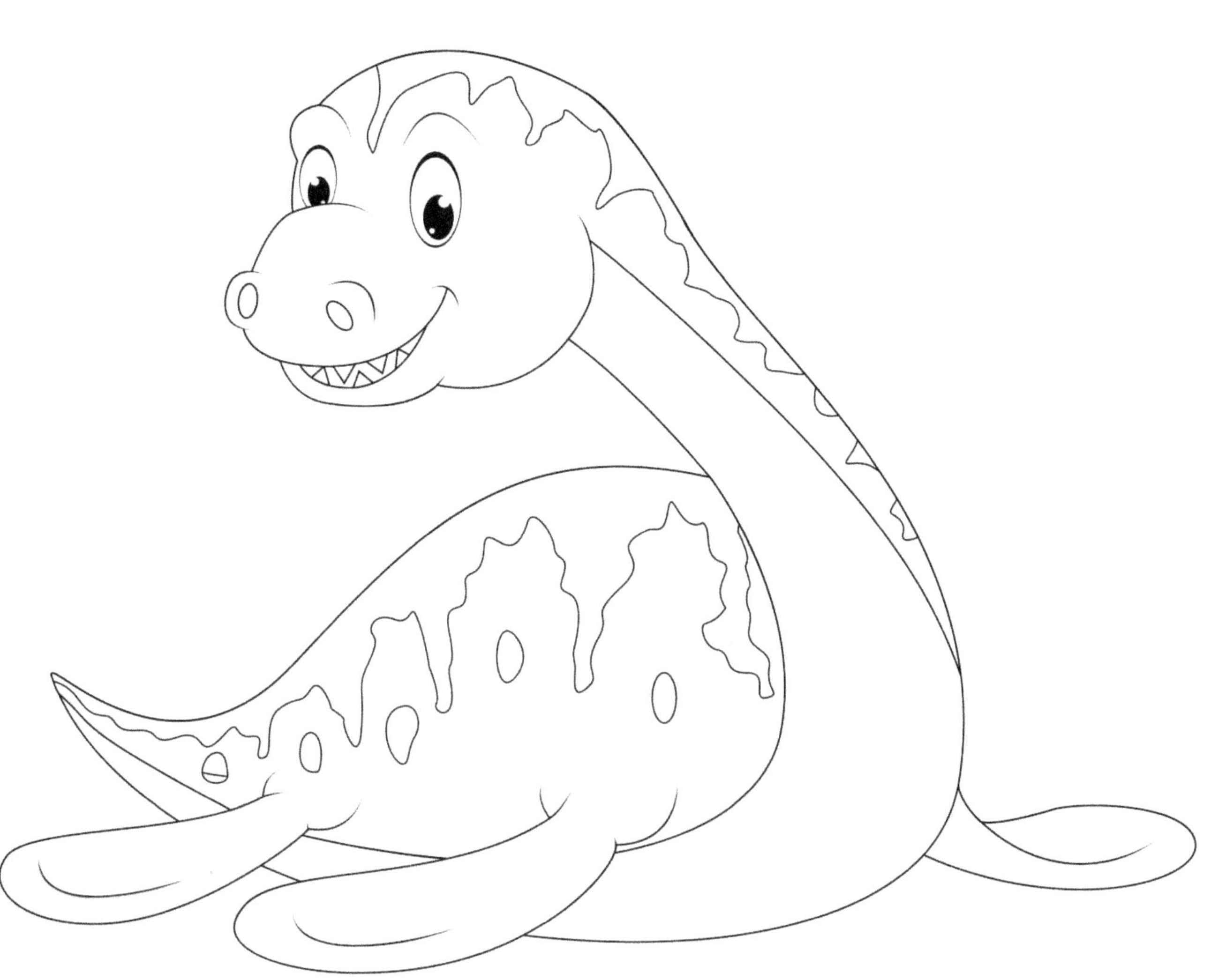

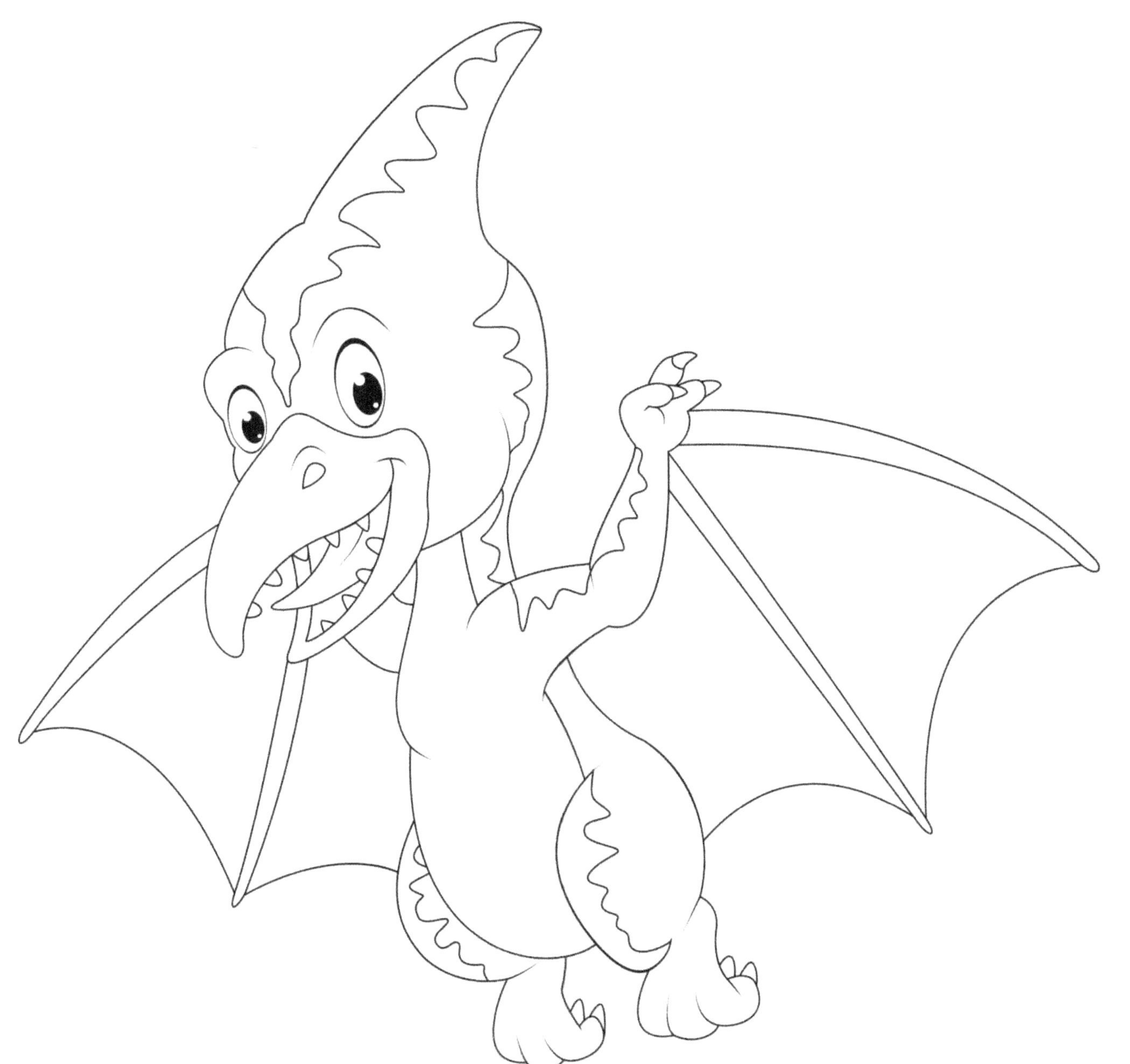

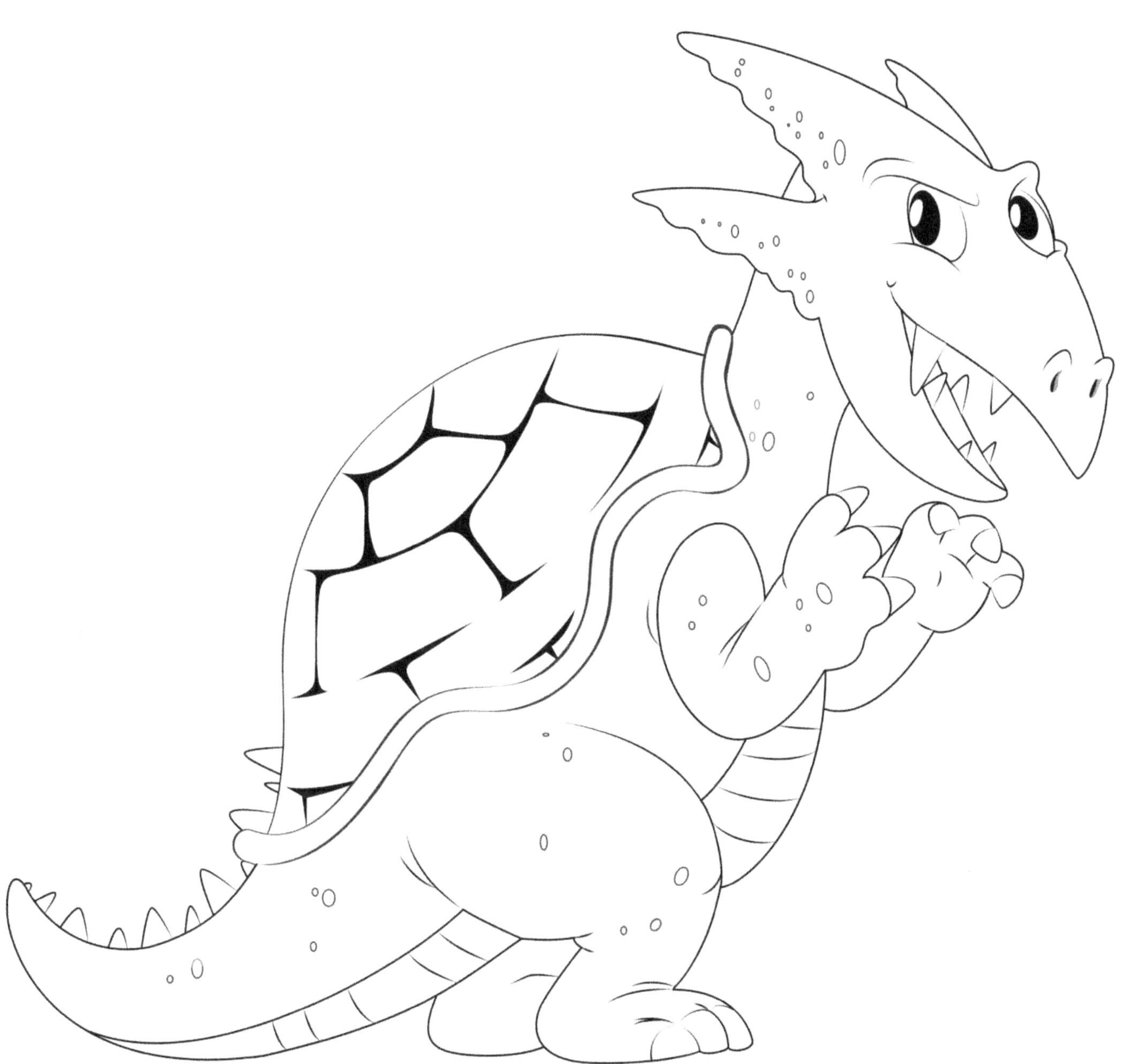

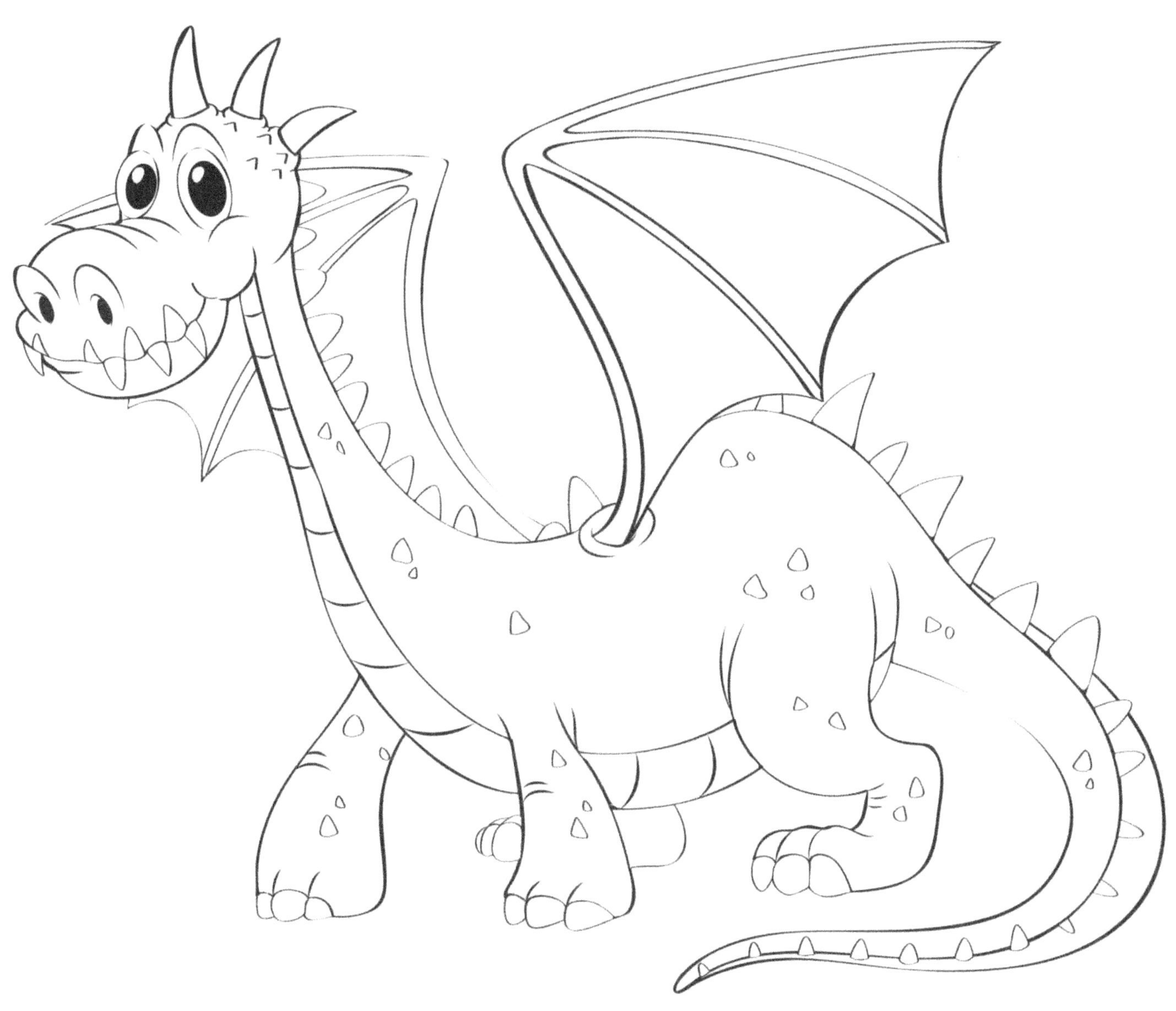

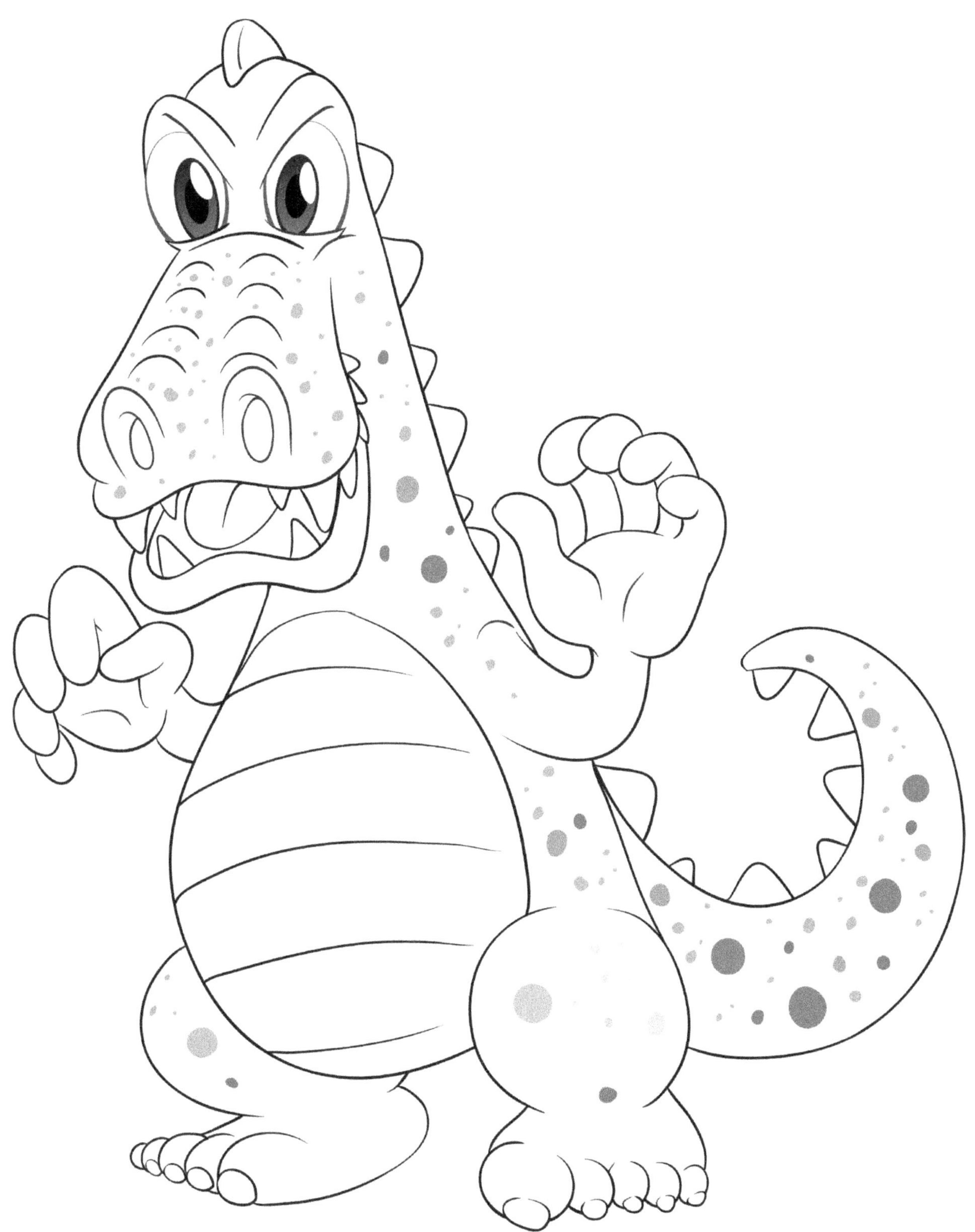

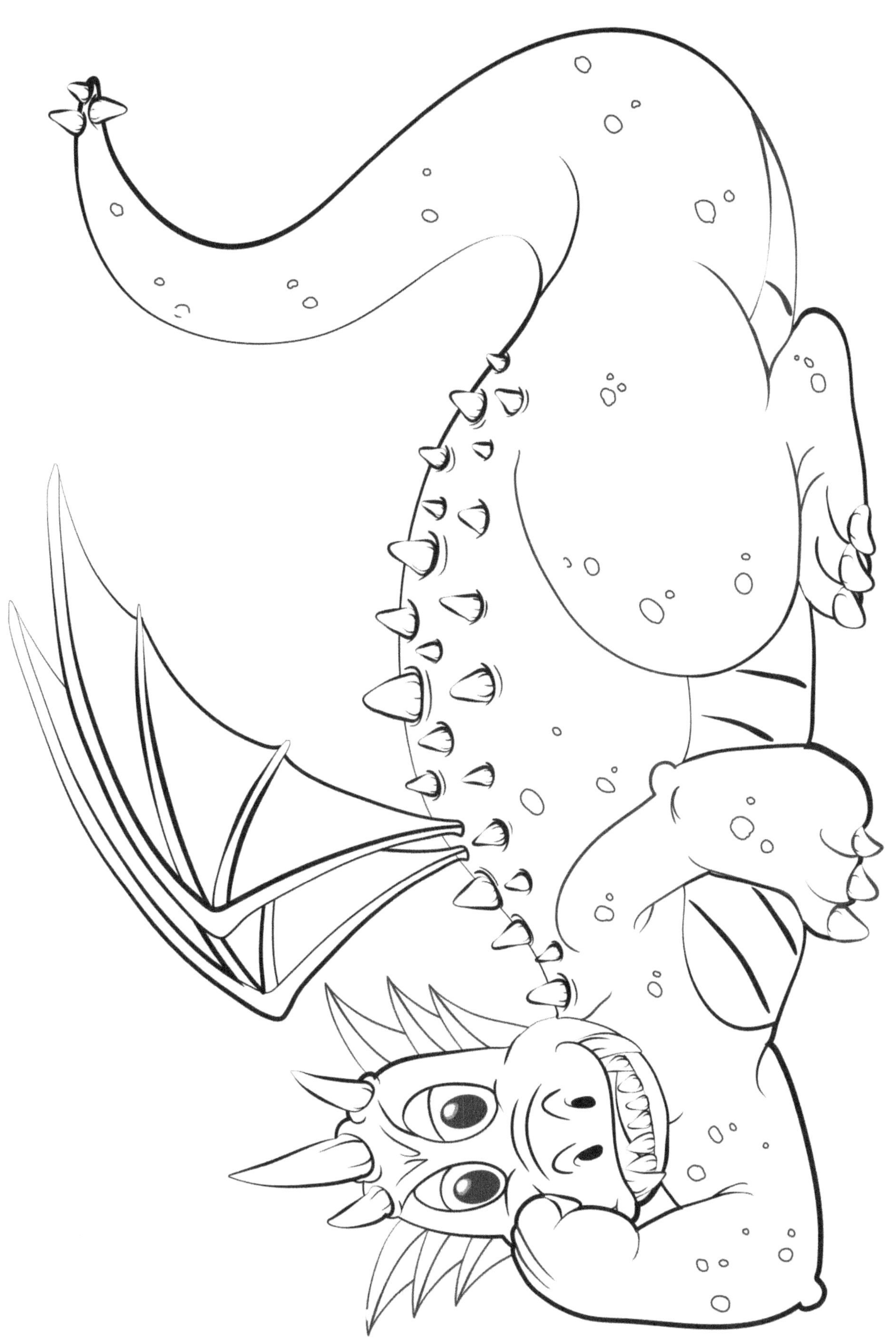

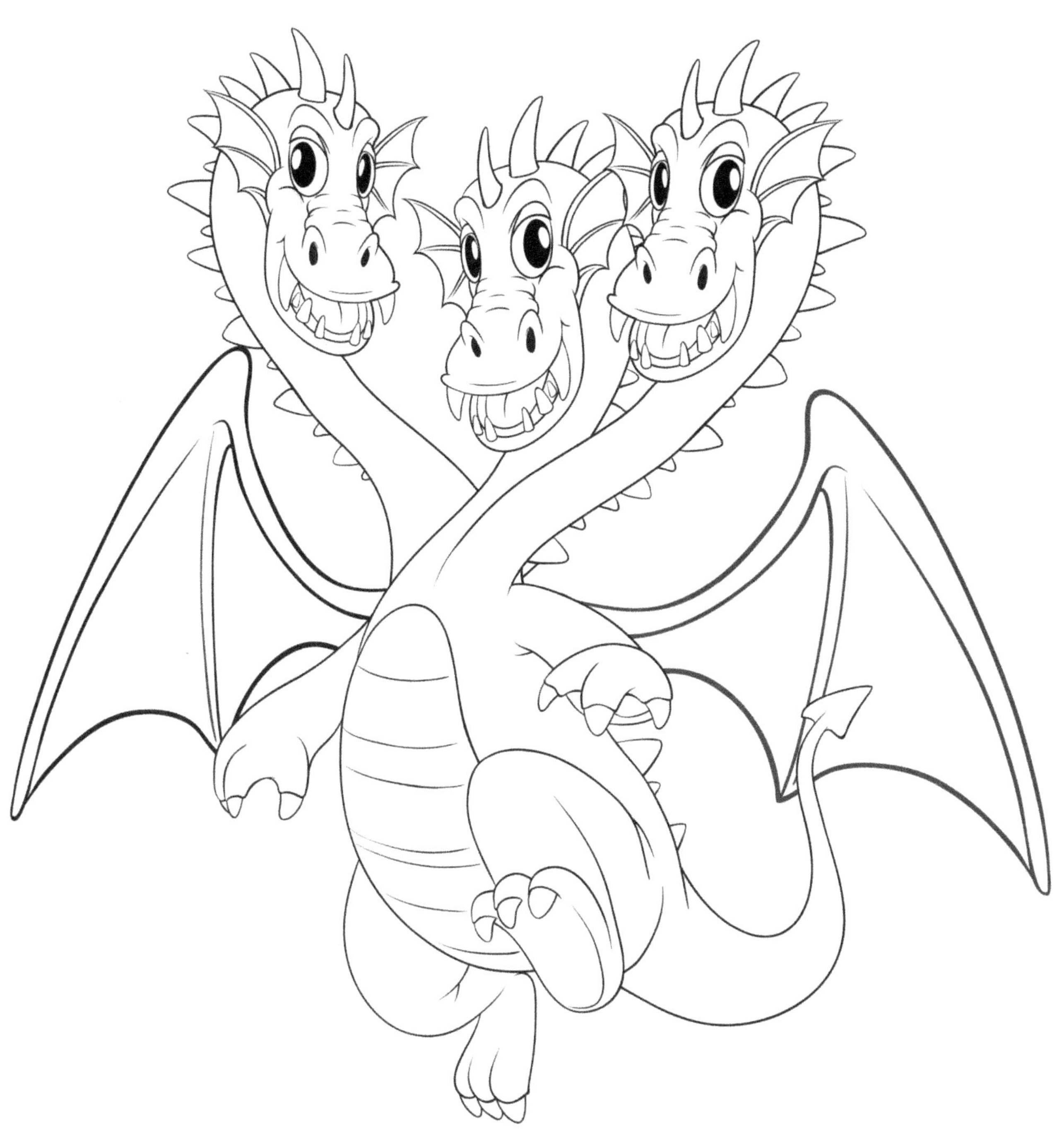

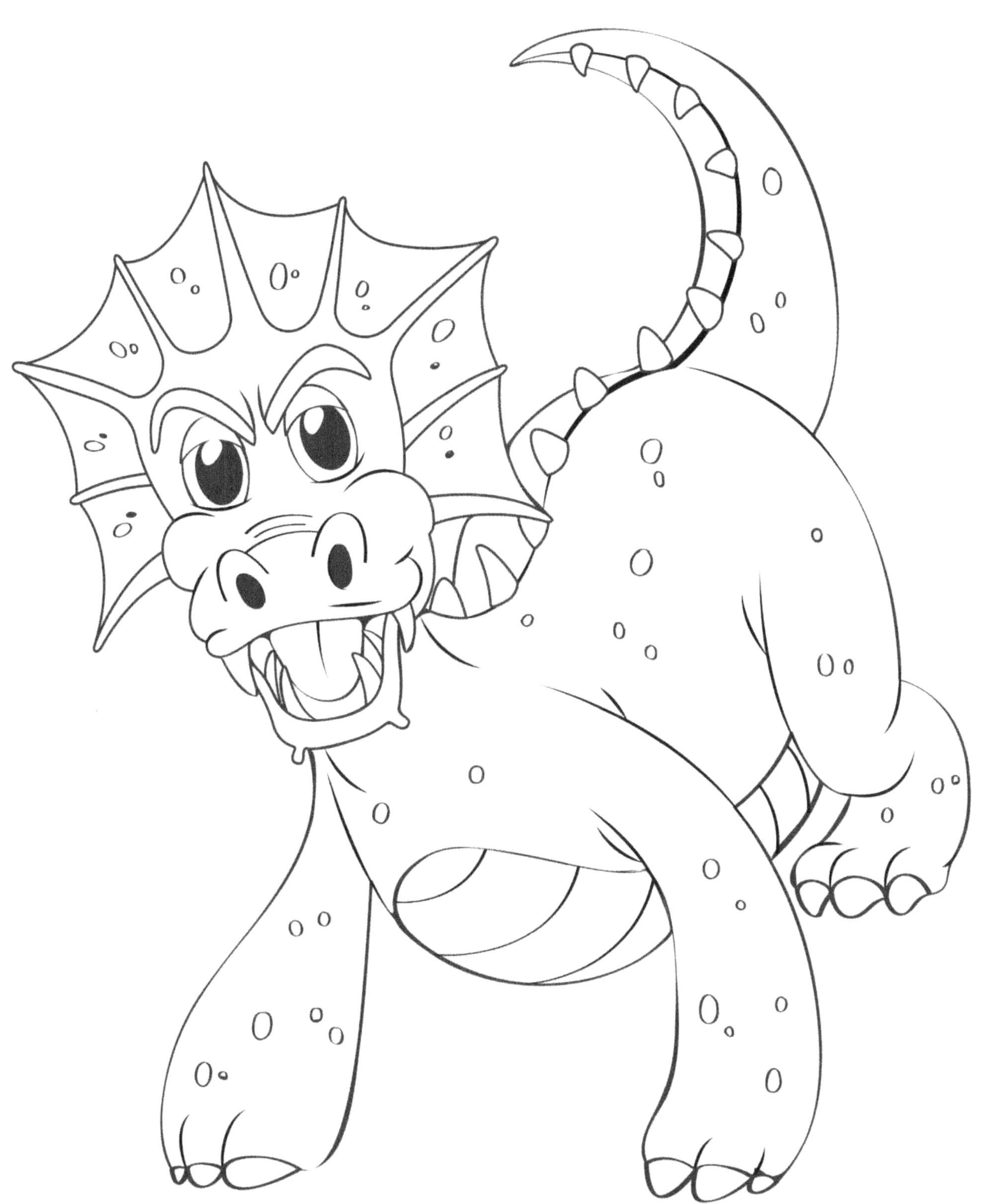

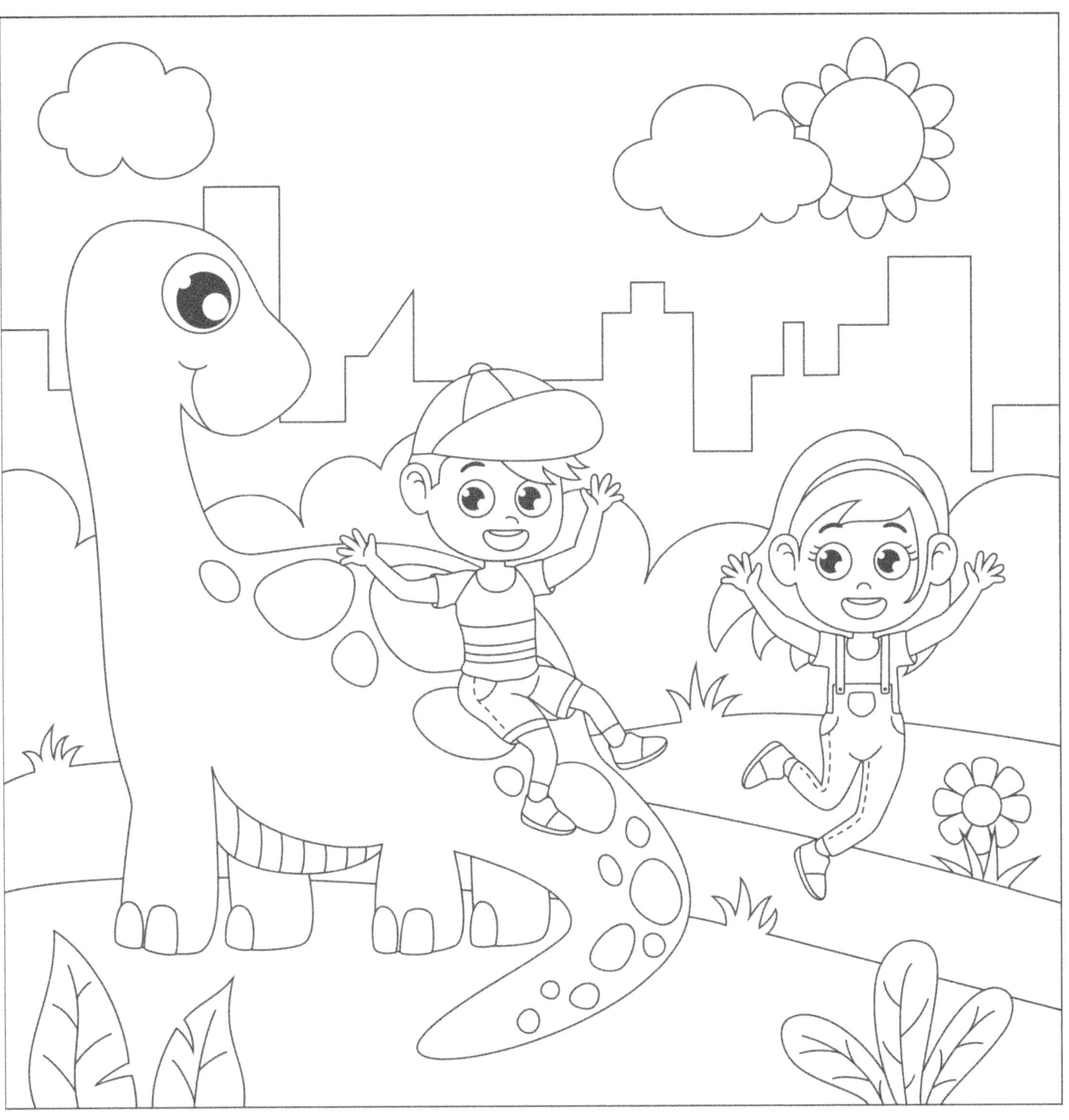

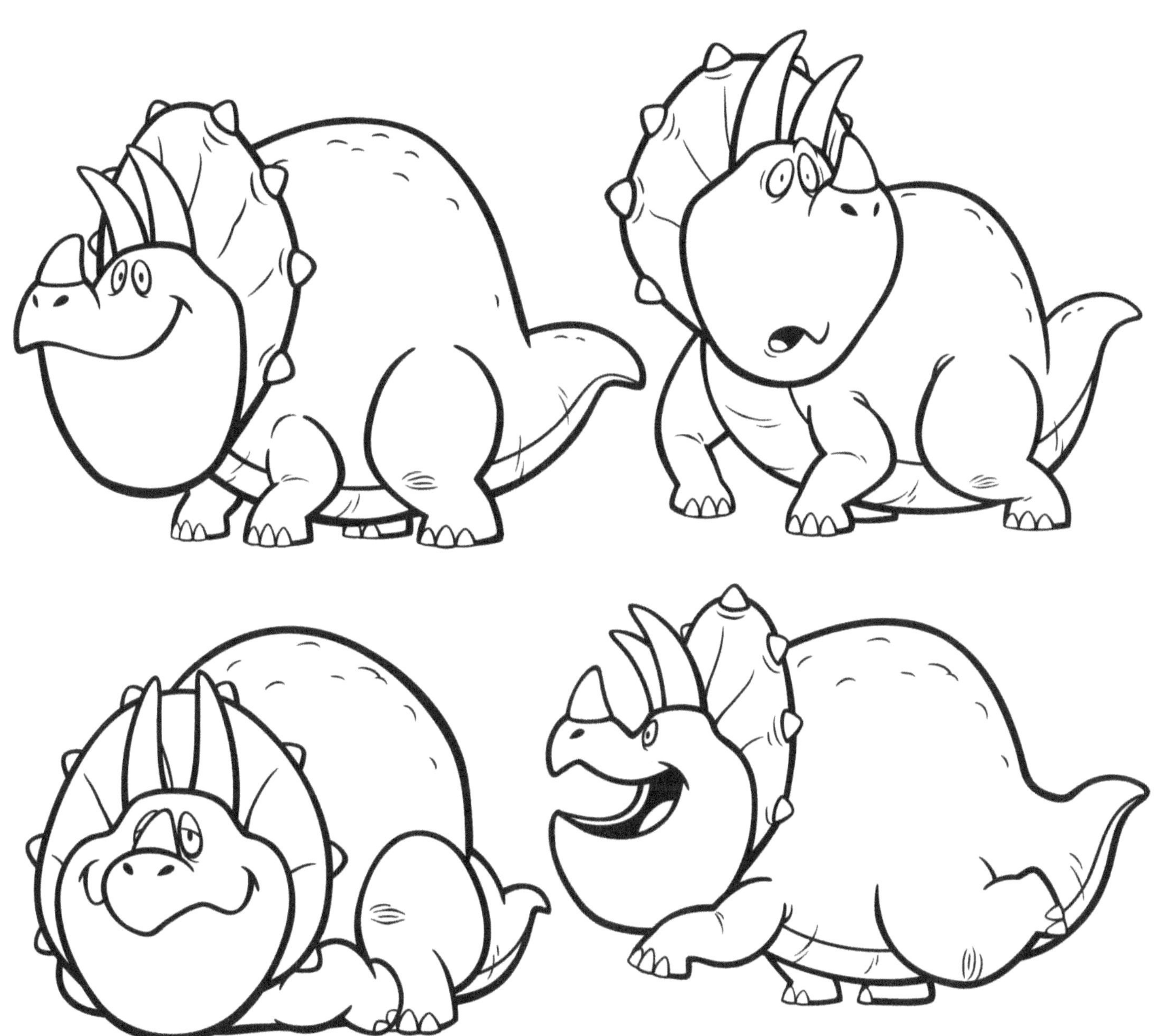

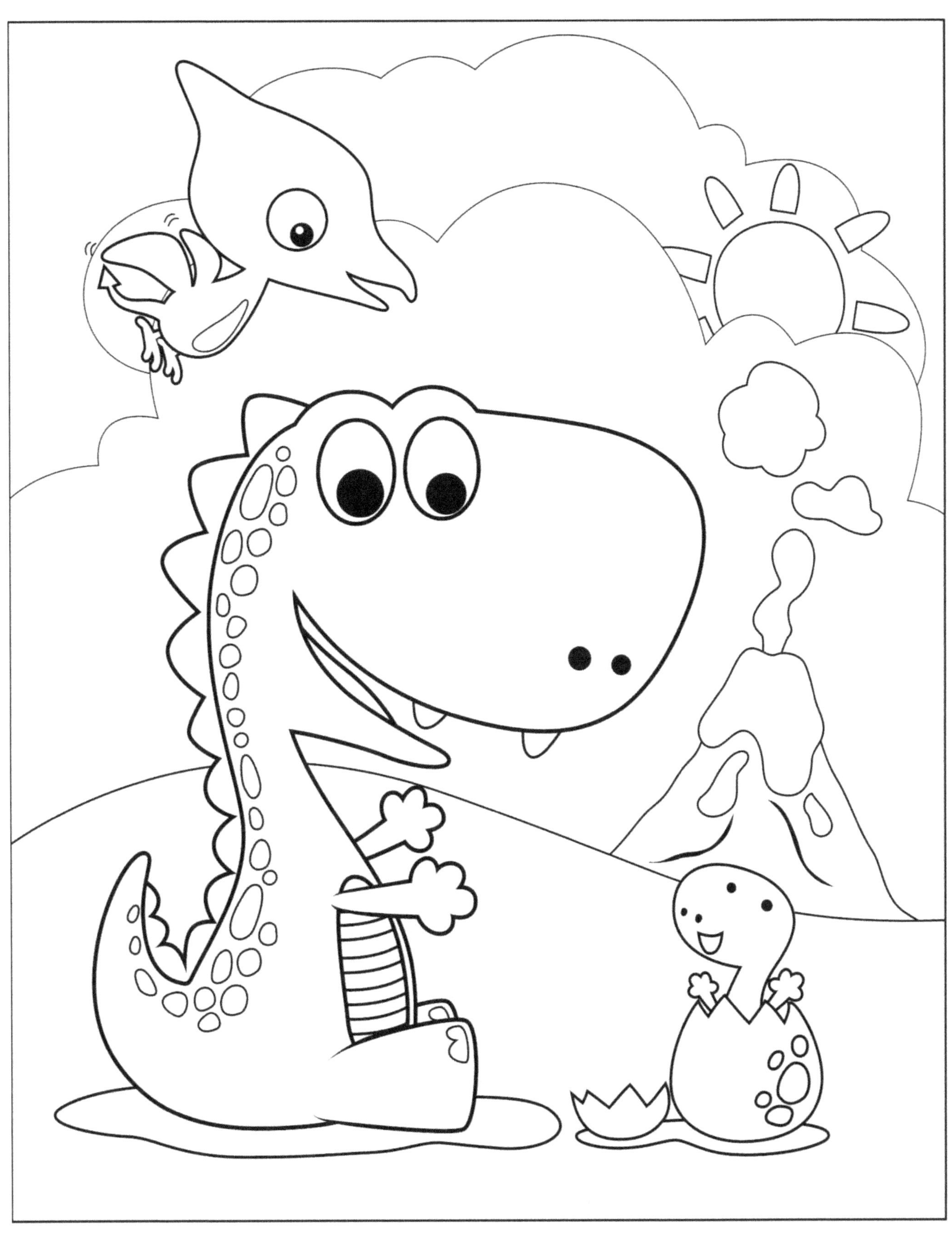

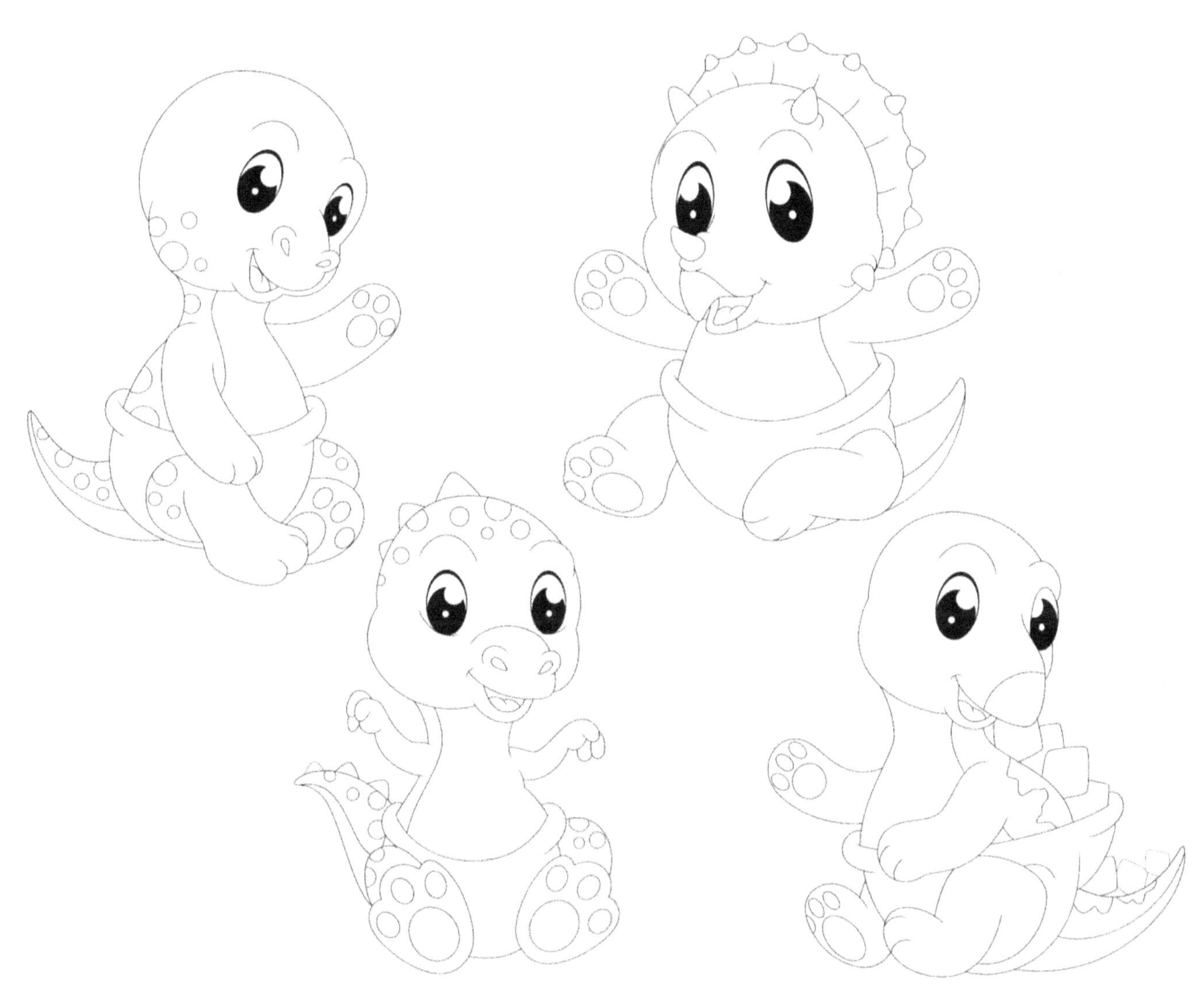

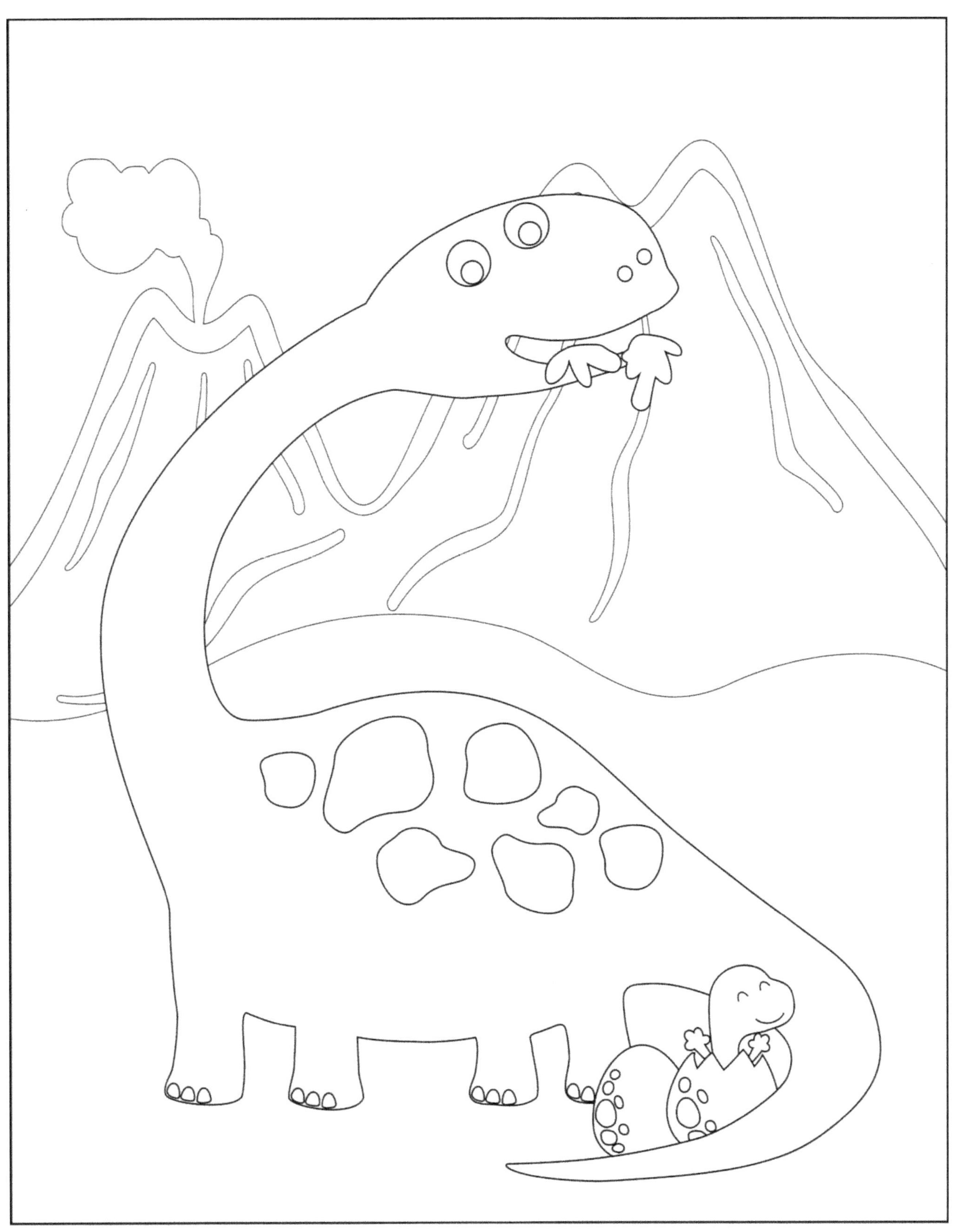

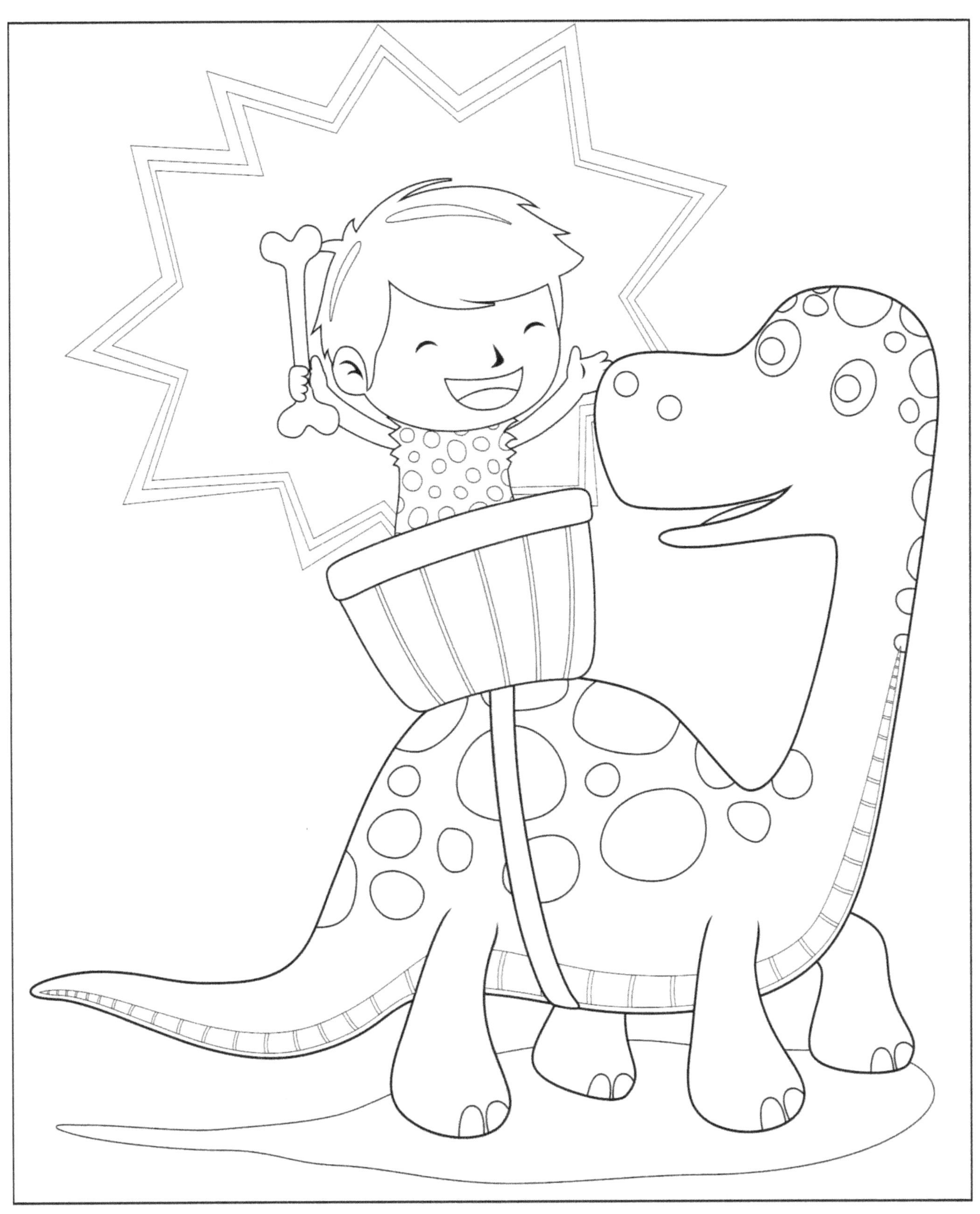

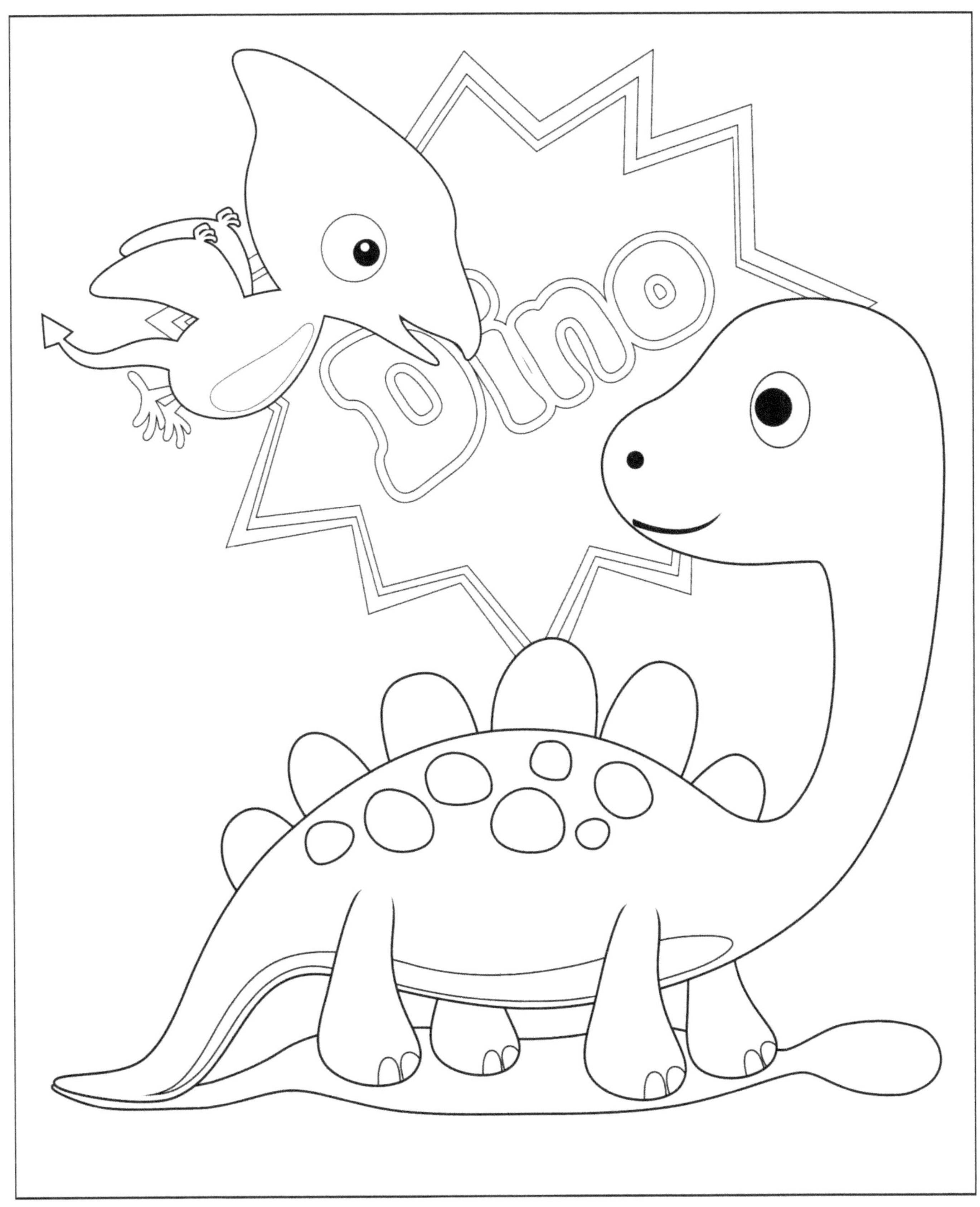
Dino

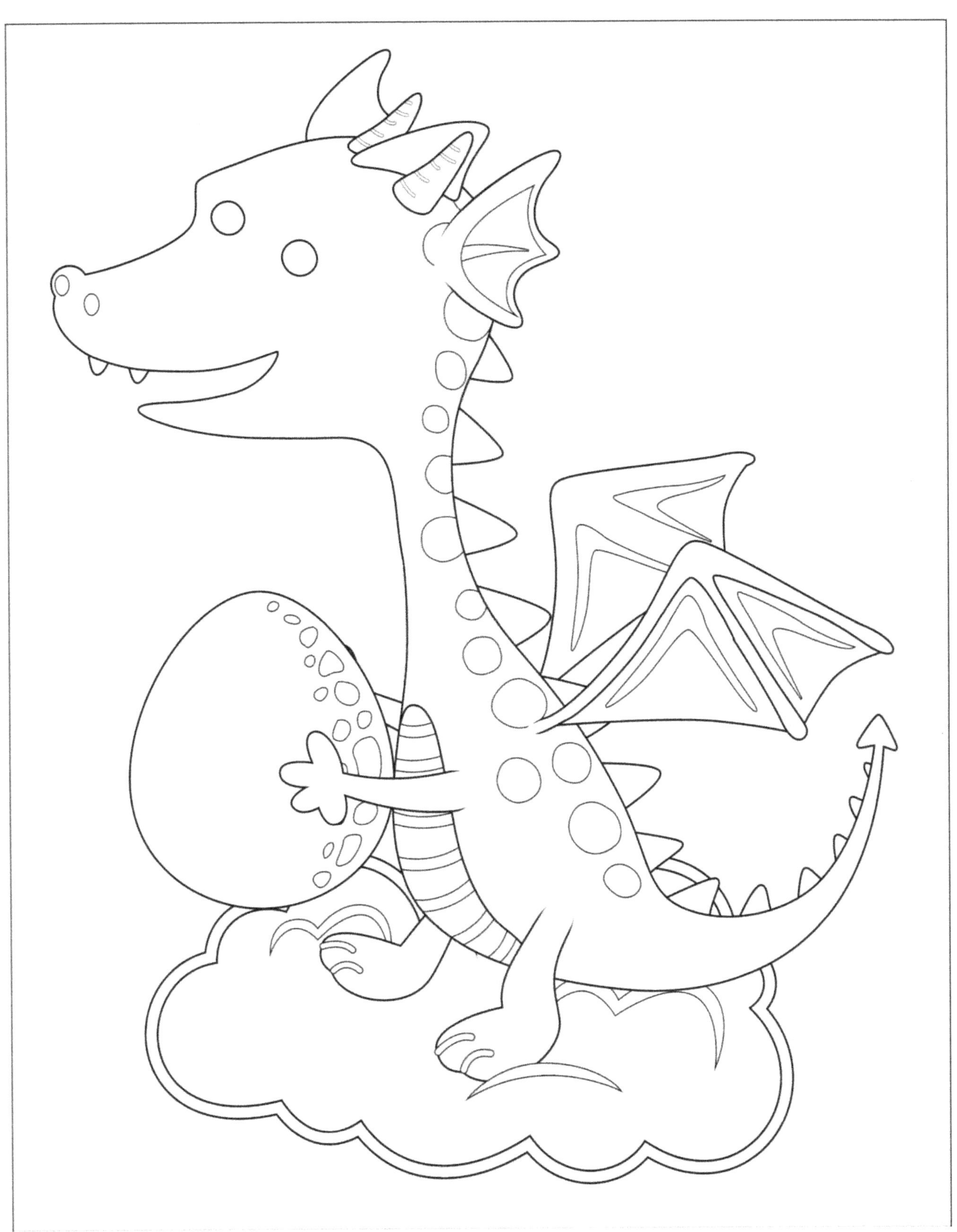

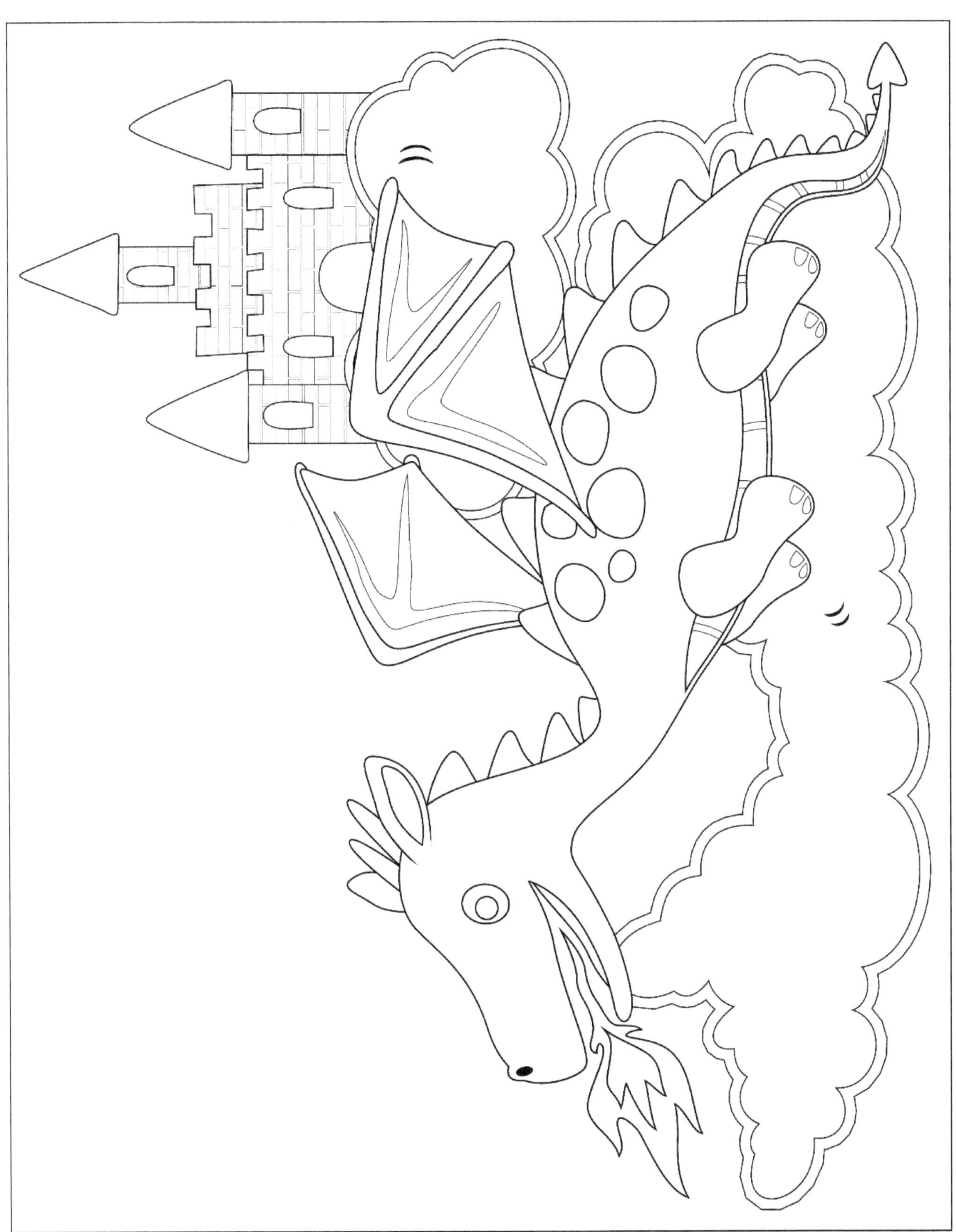

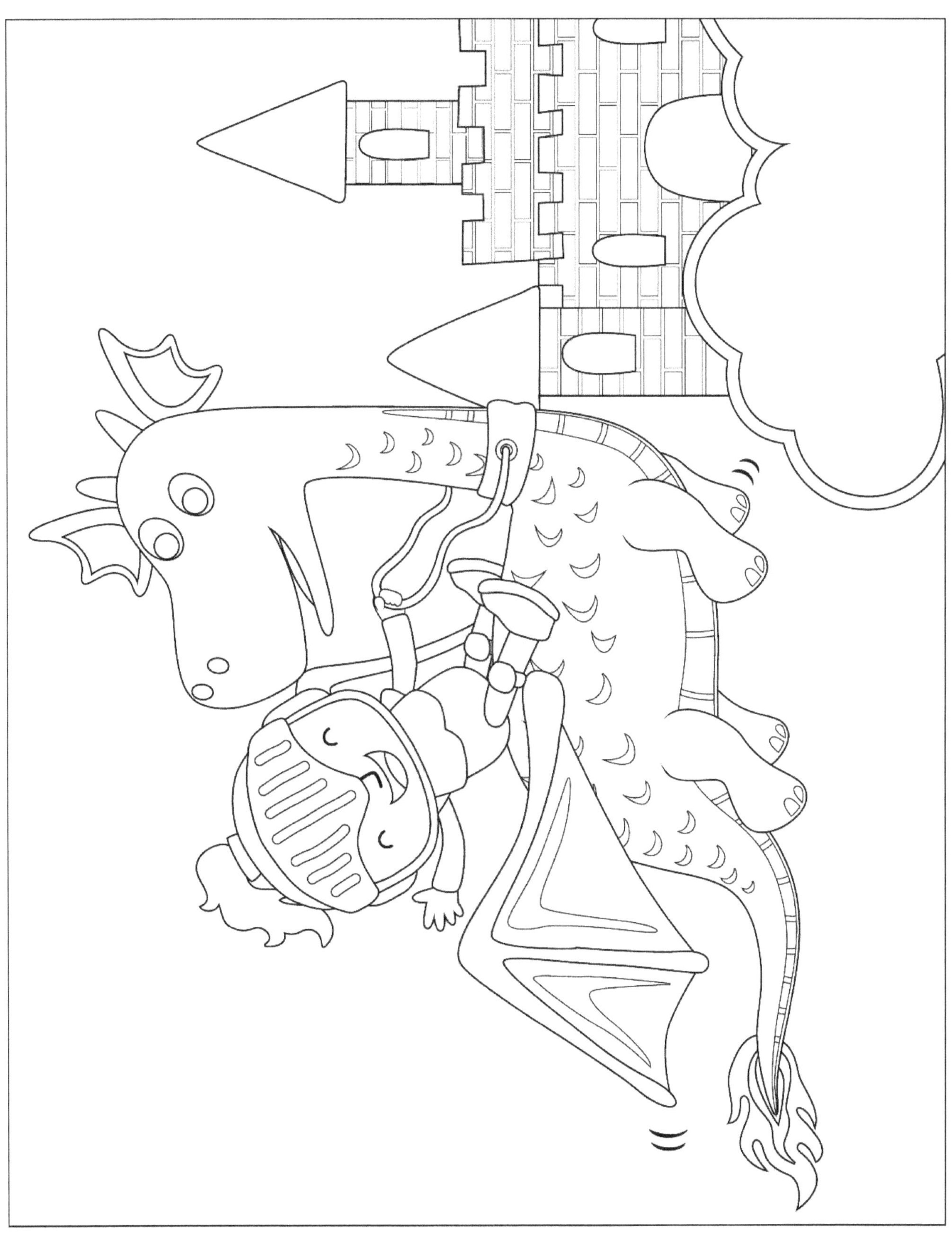

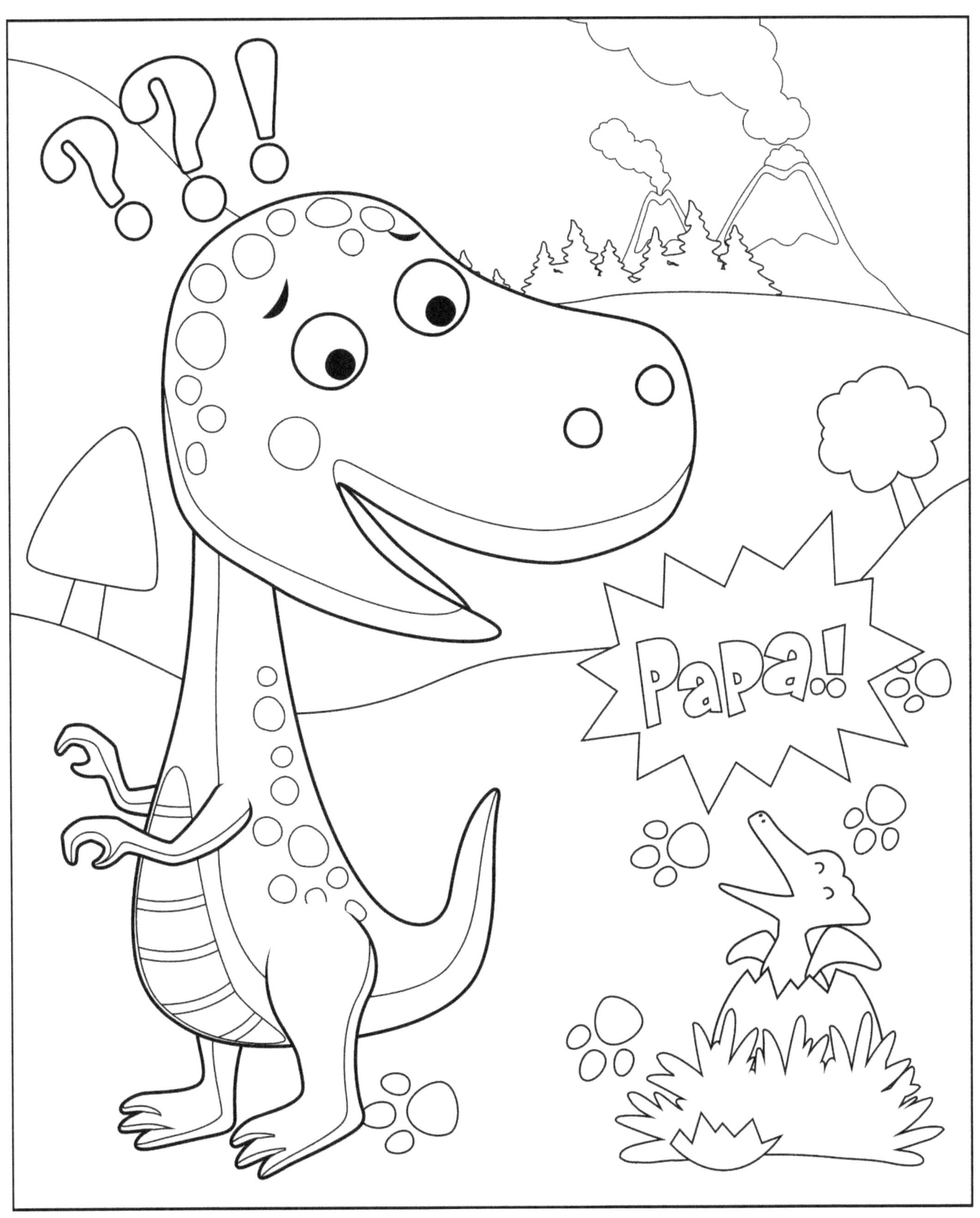

PaPa!!

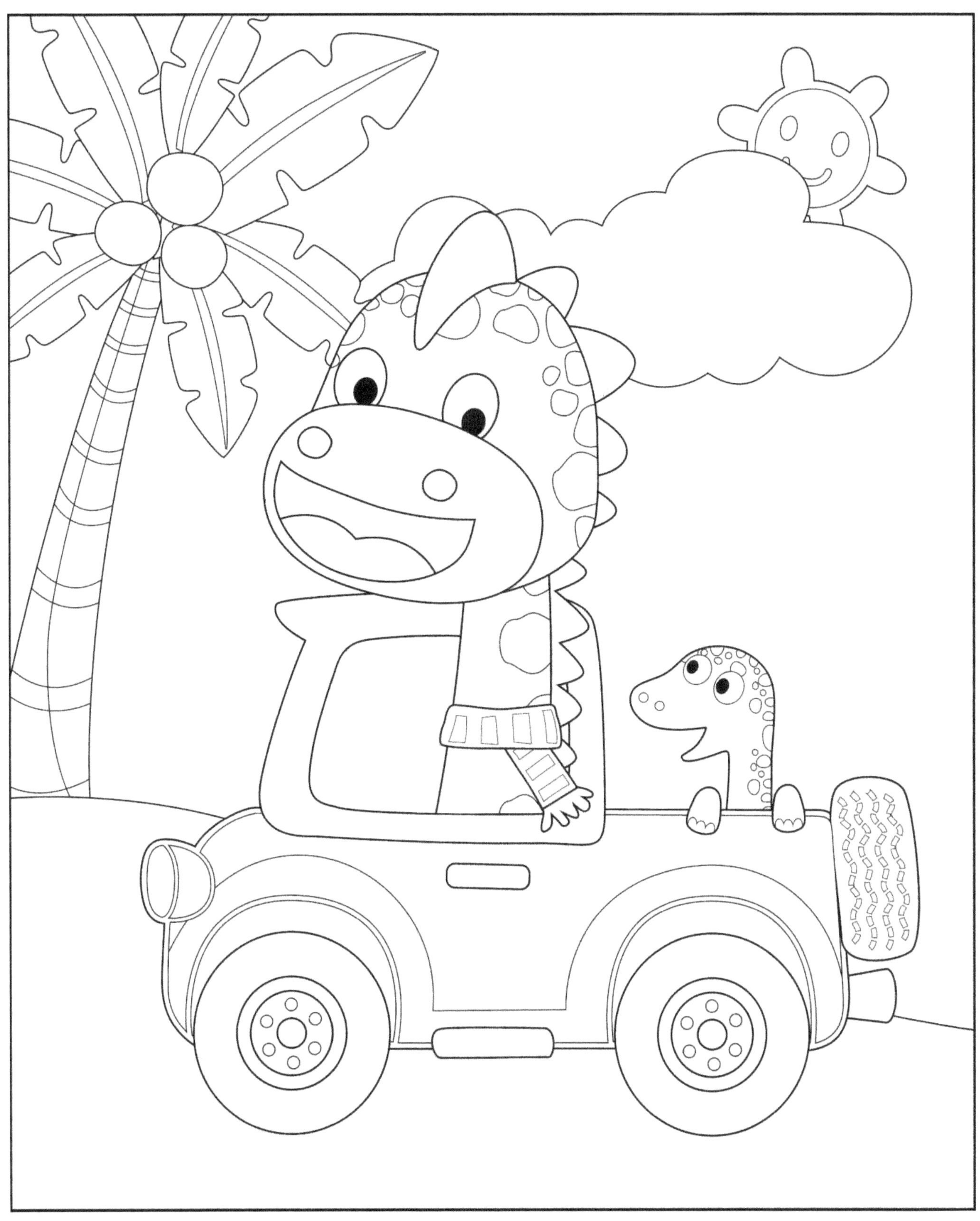

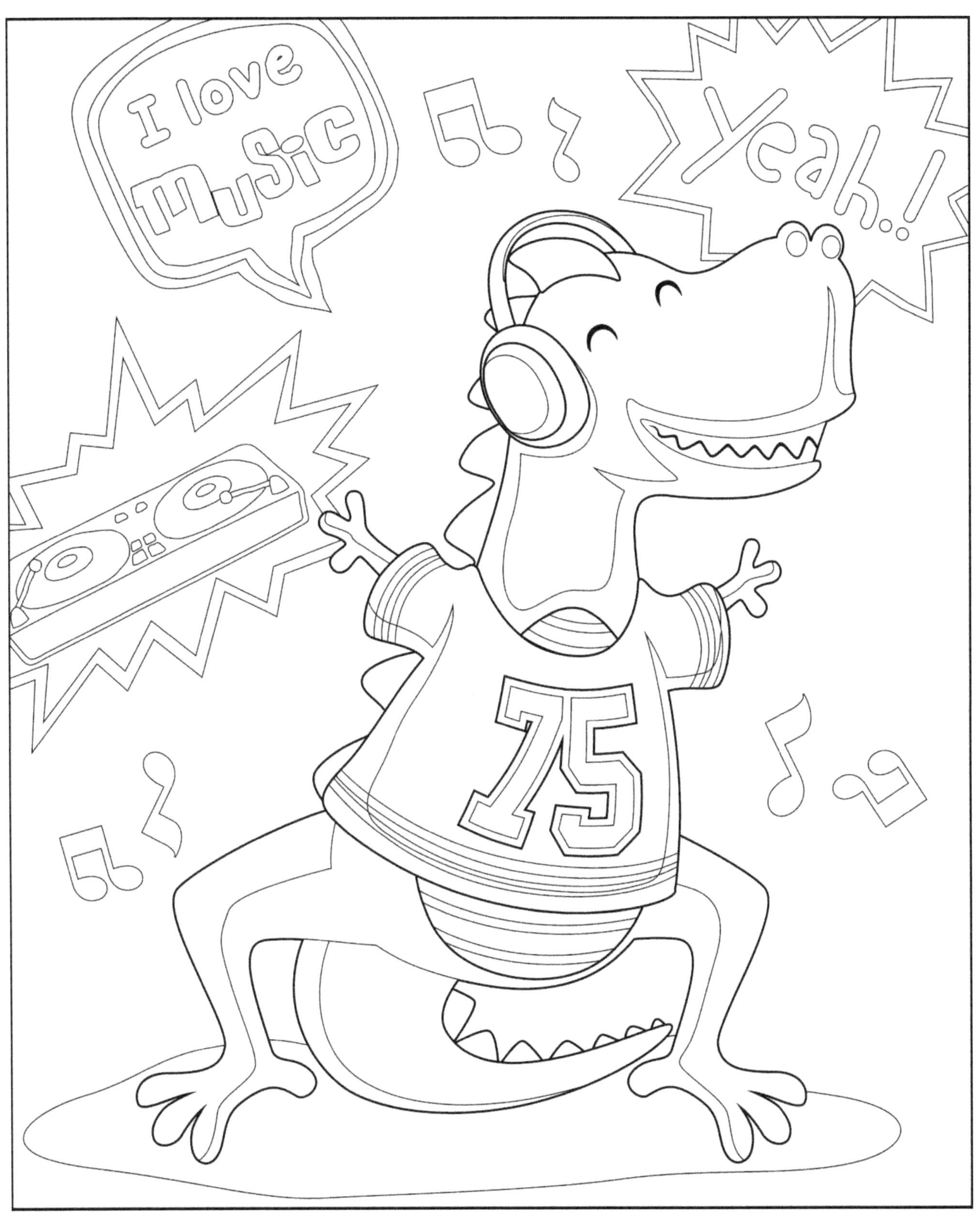

I love MuSiC
Yeah..!
75

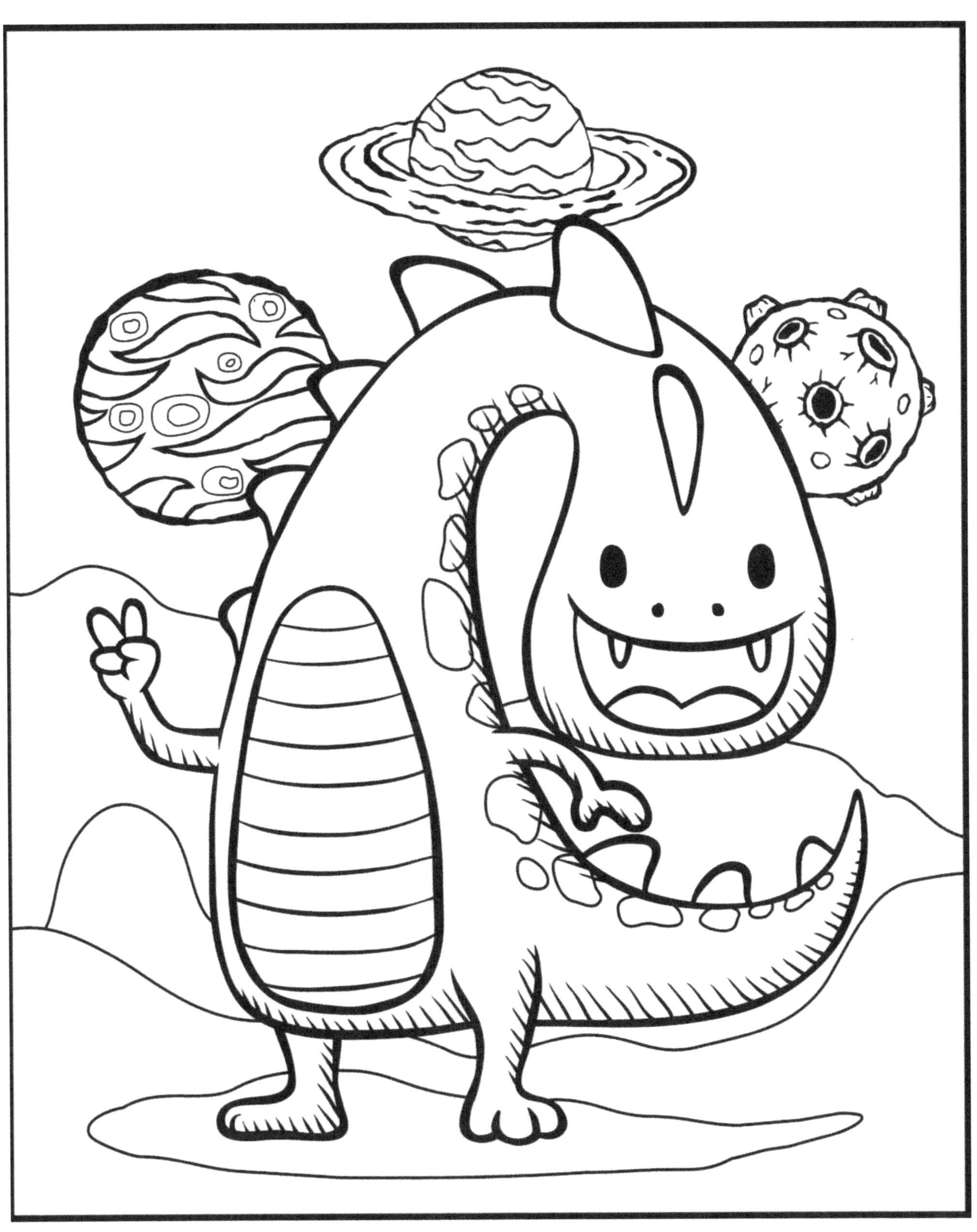

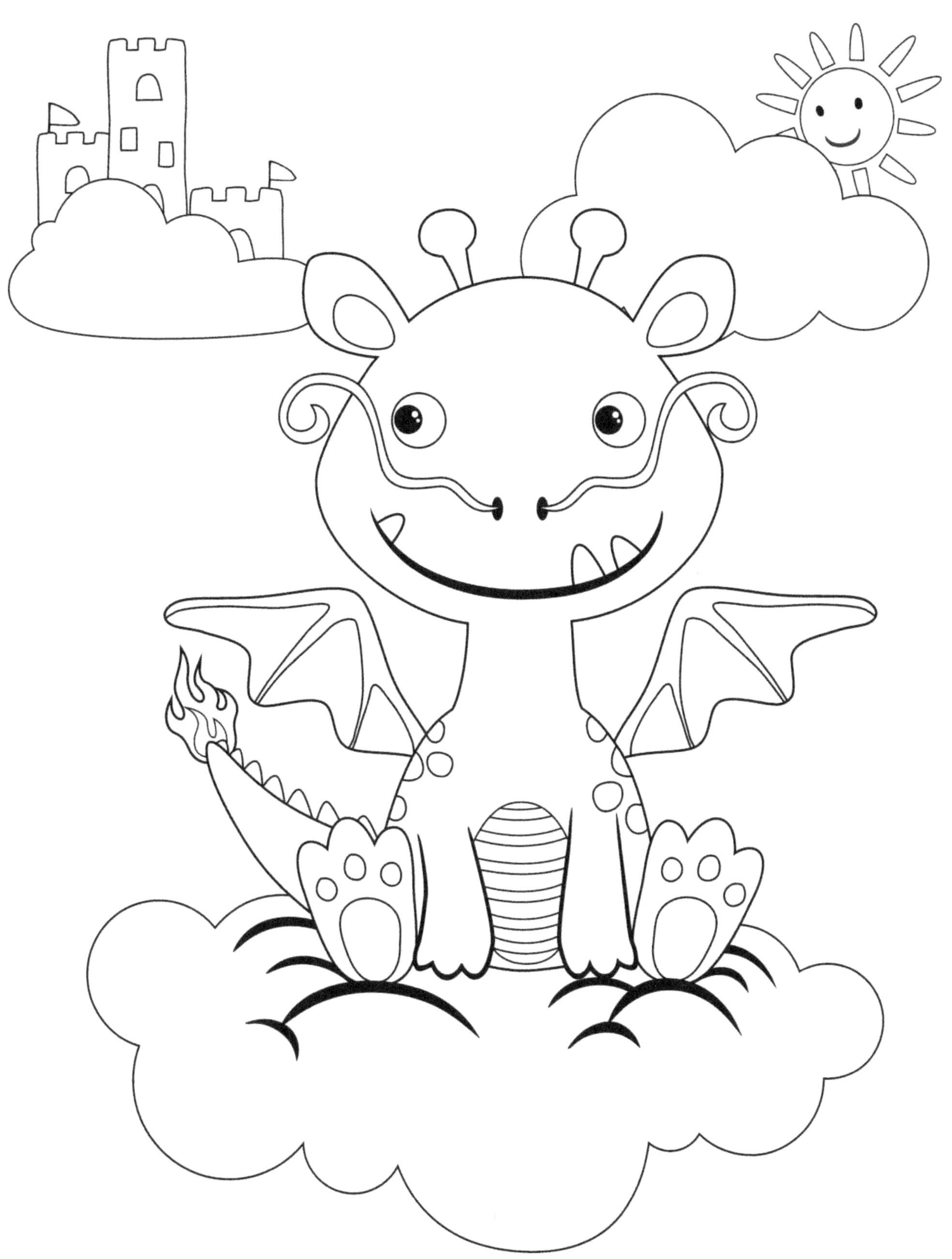

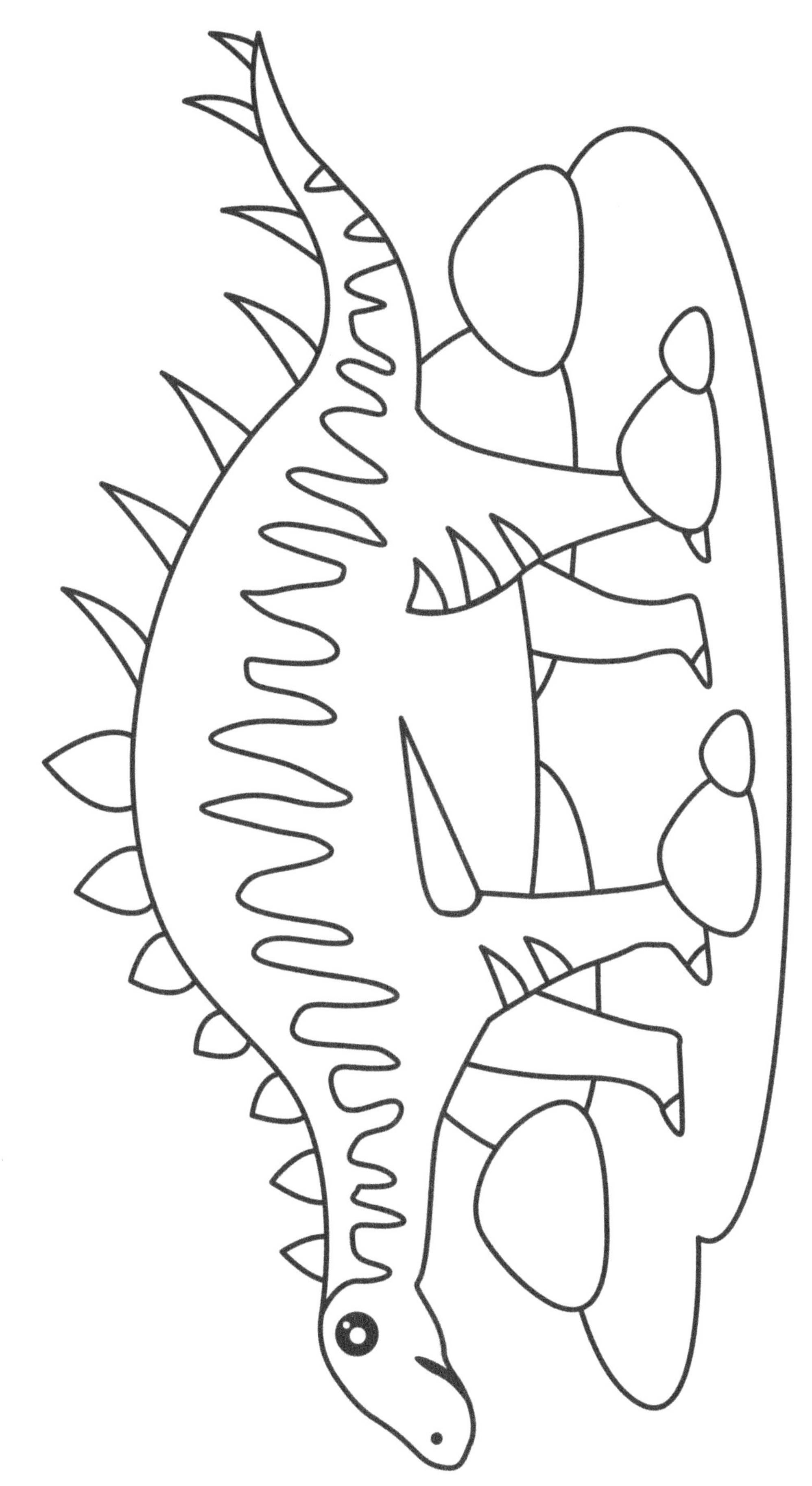

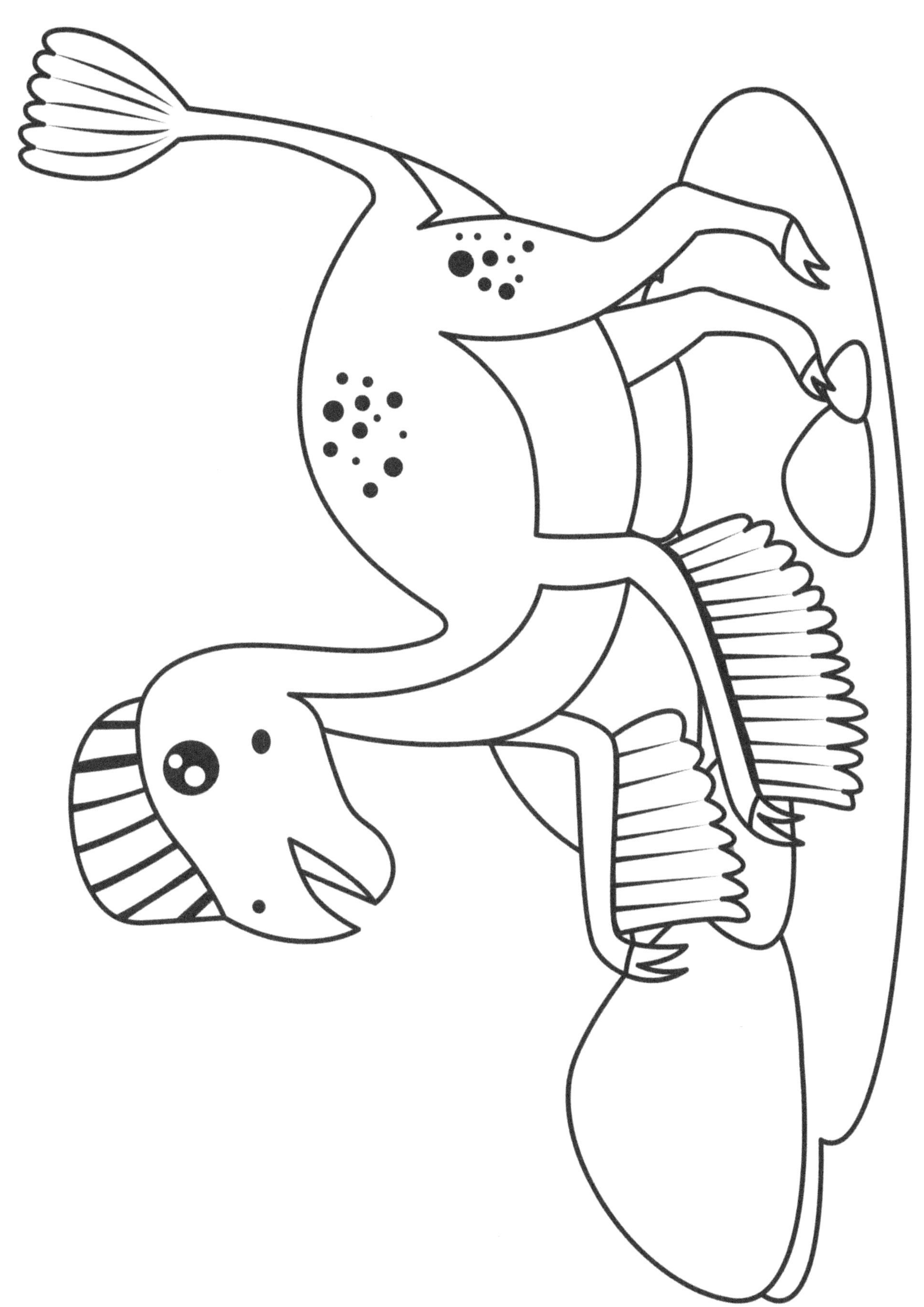

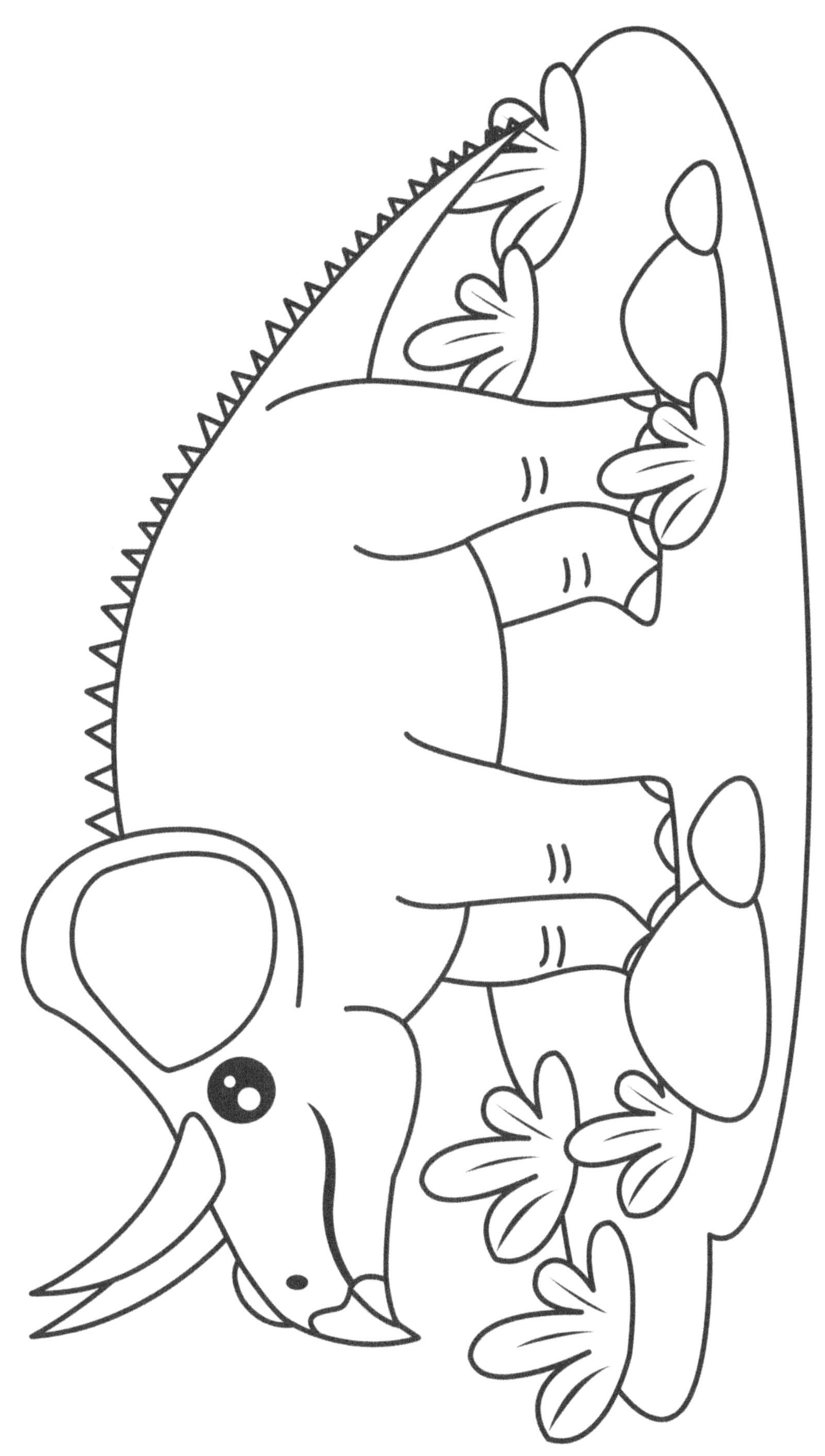

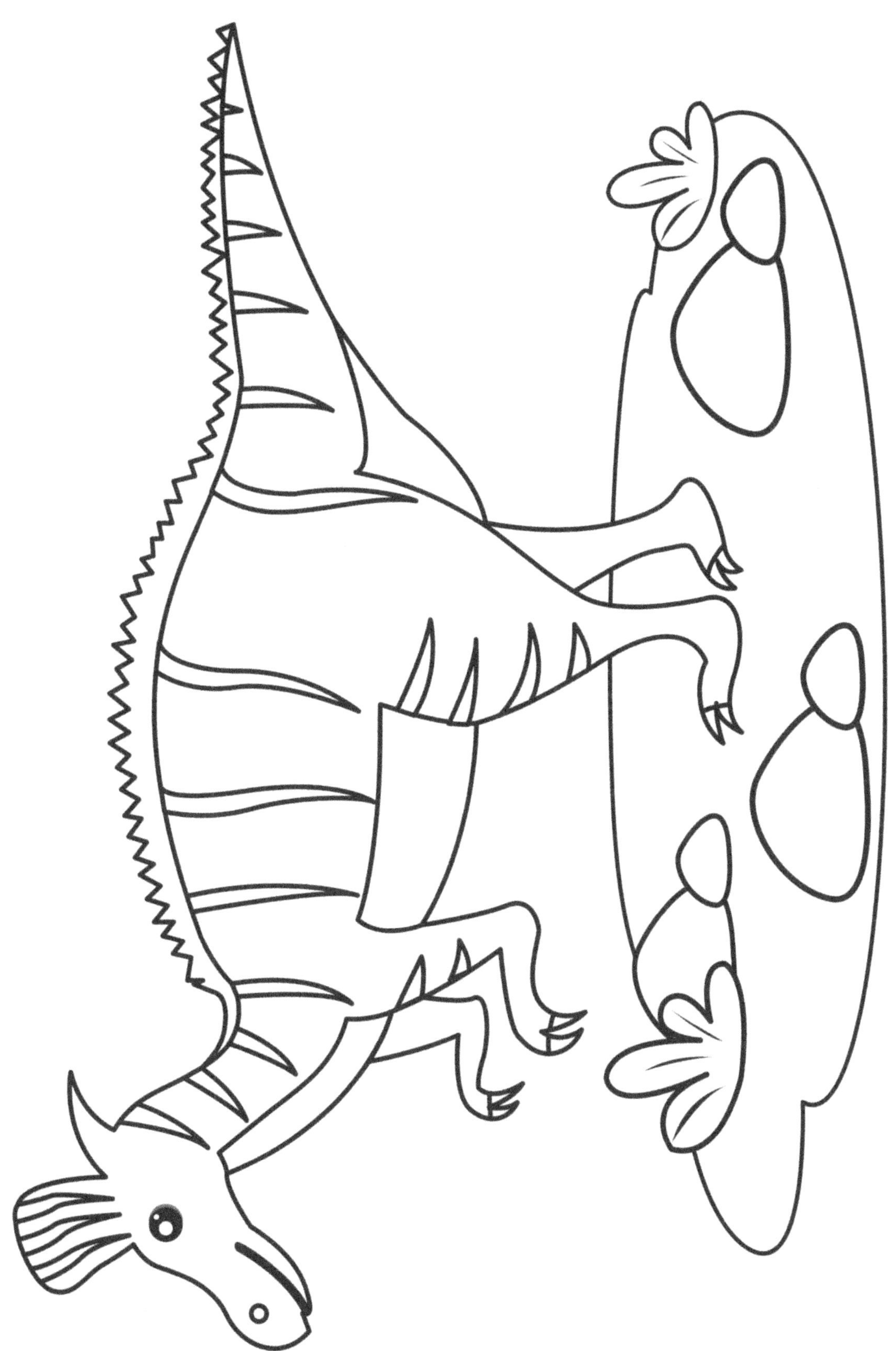

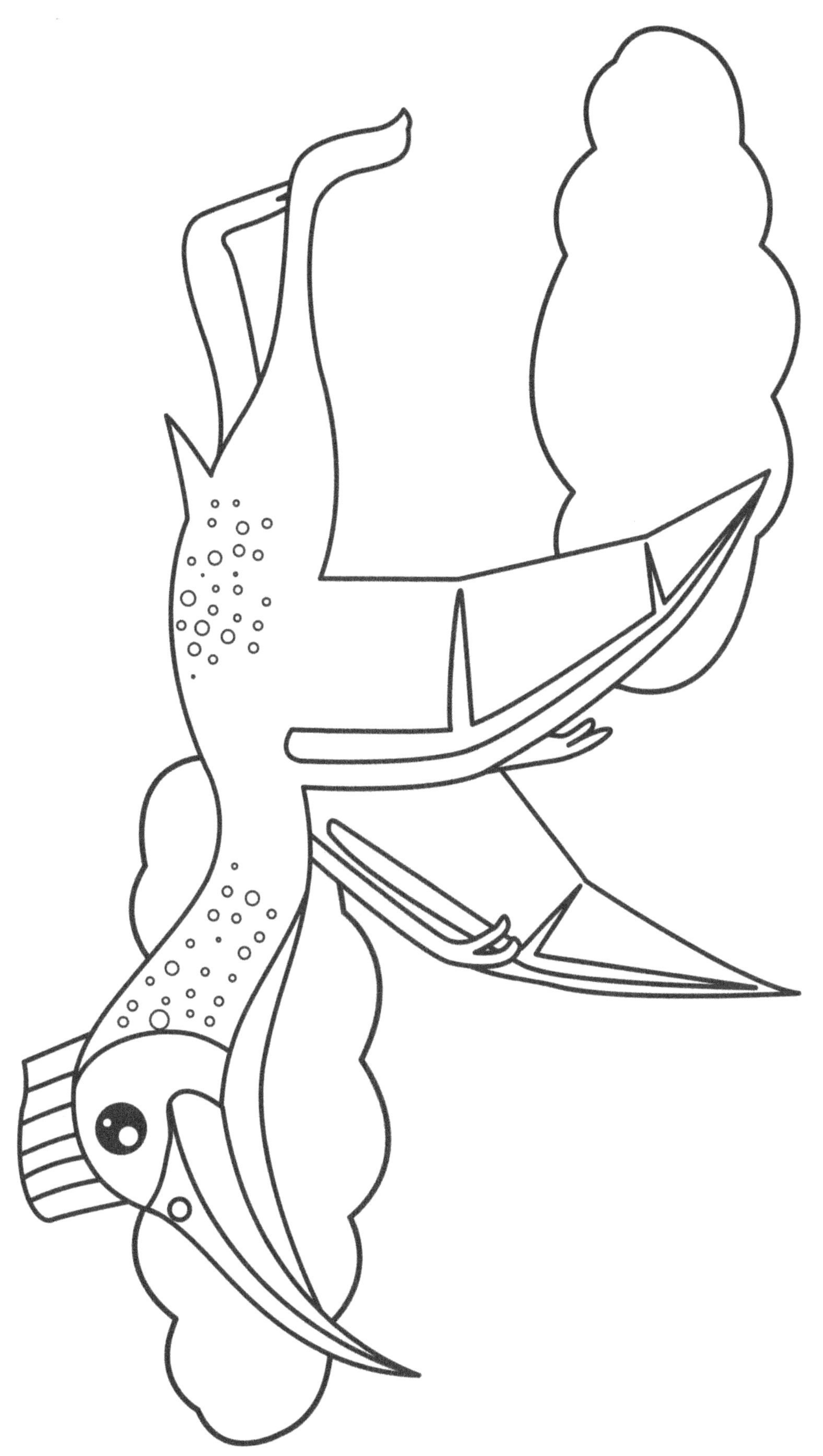

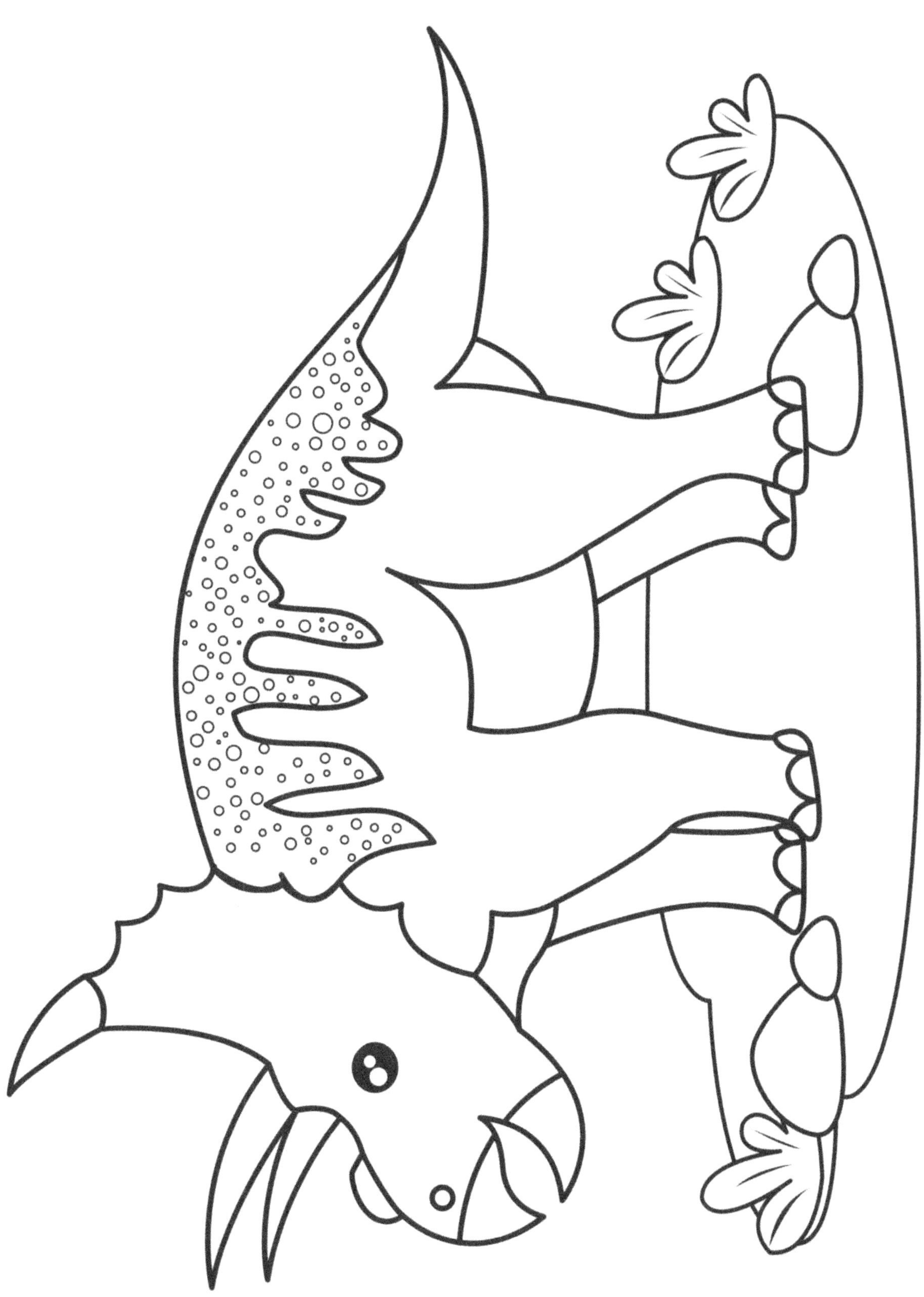

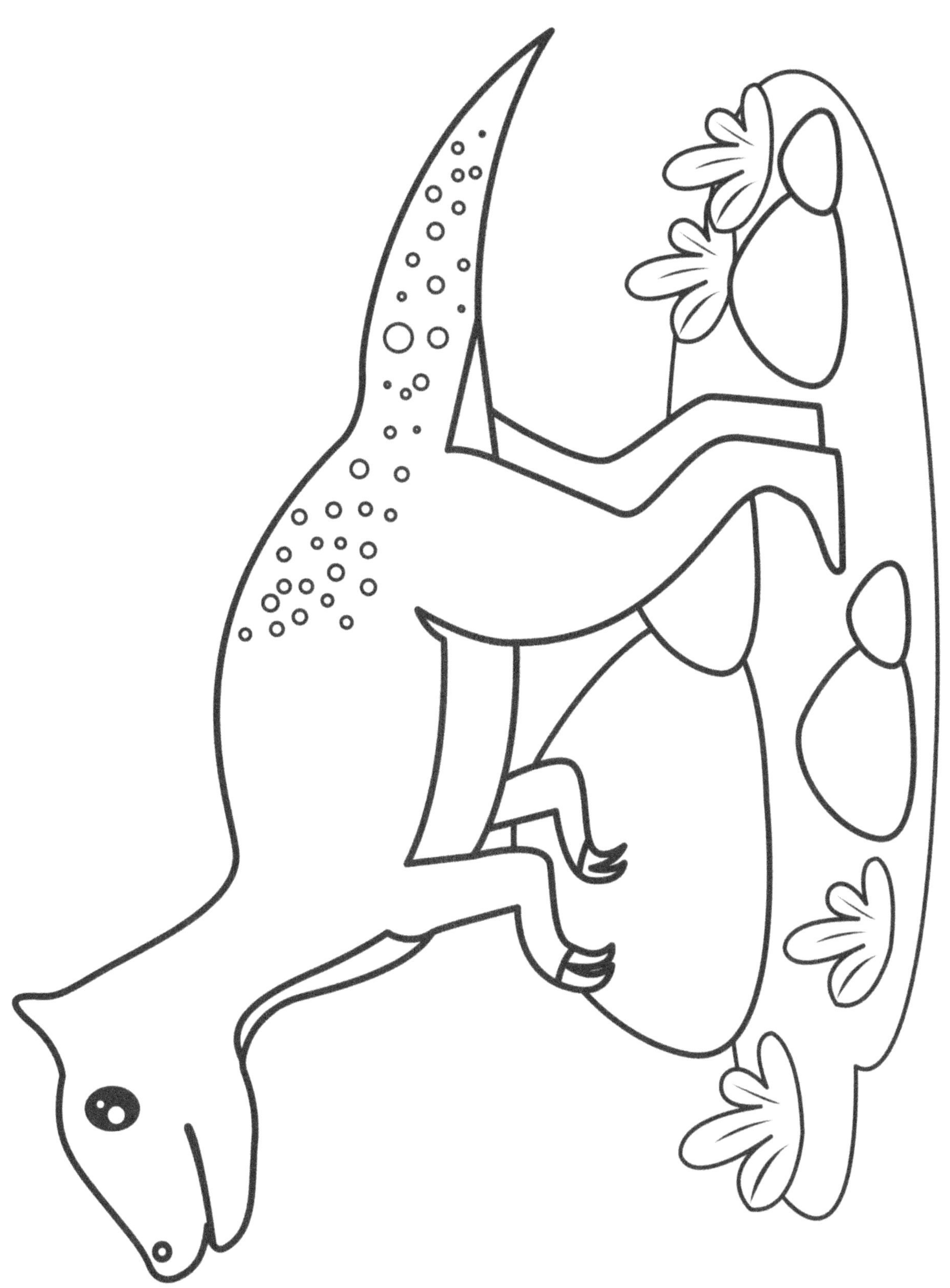

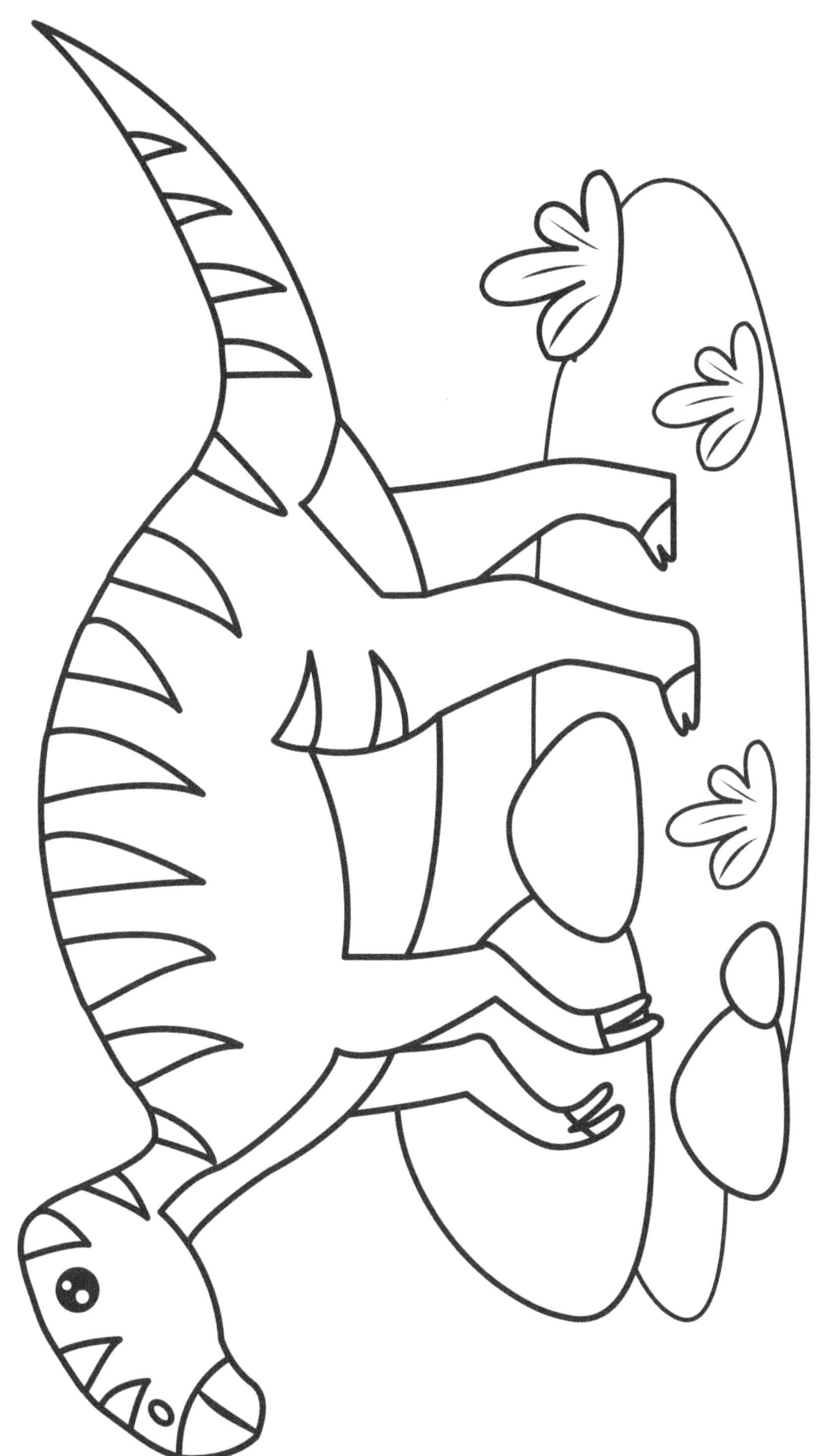

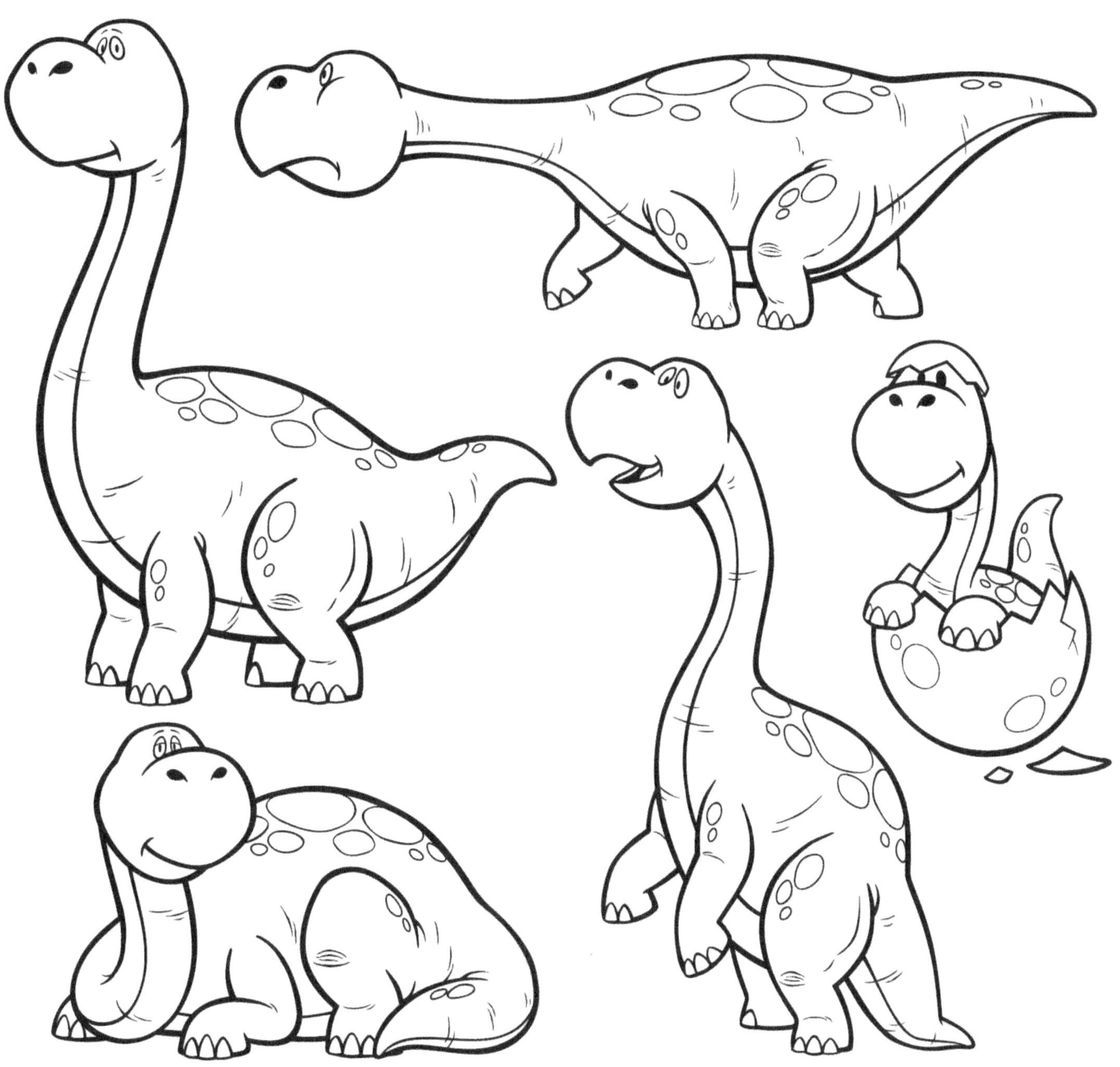

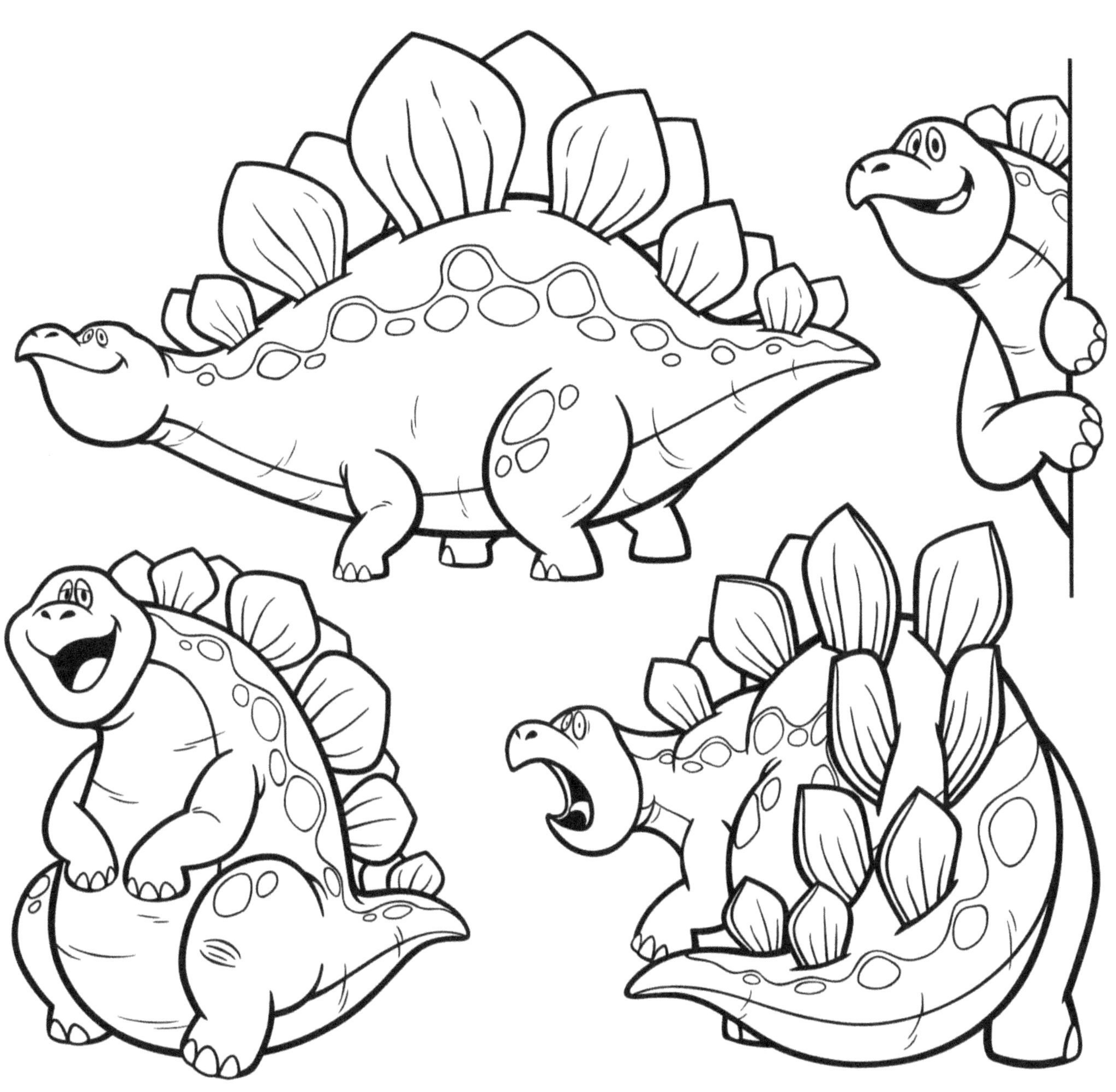

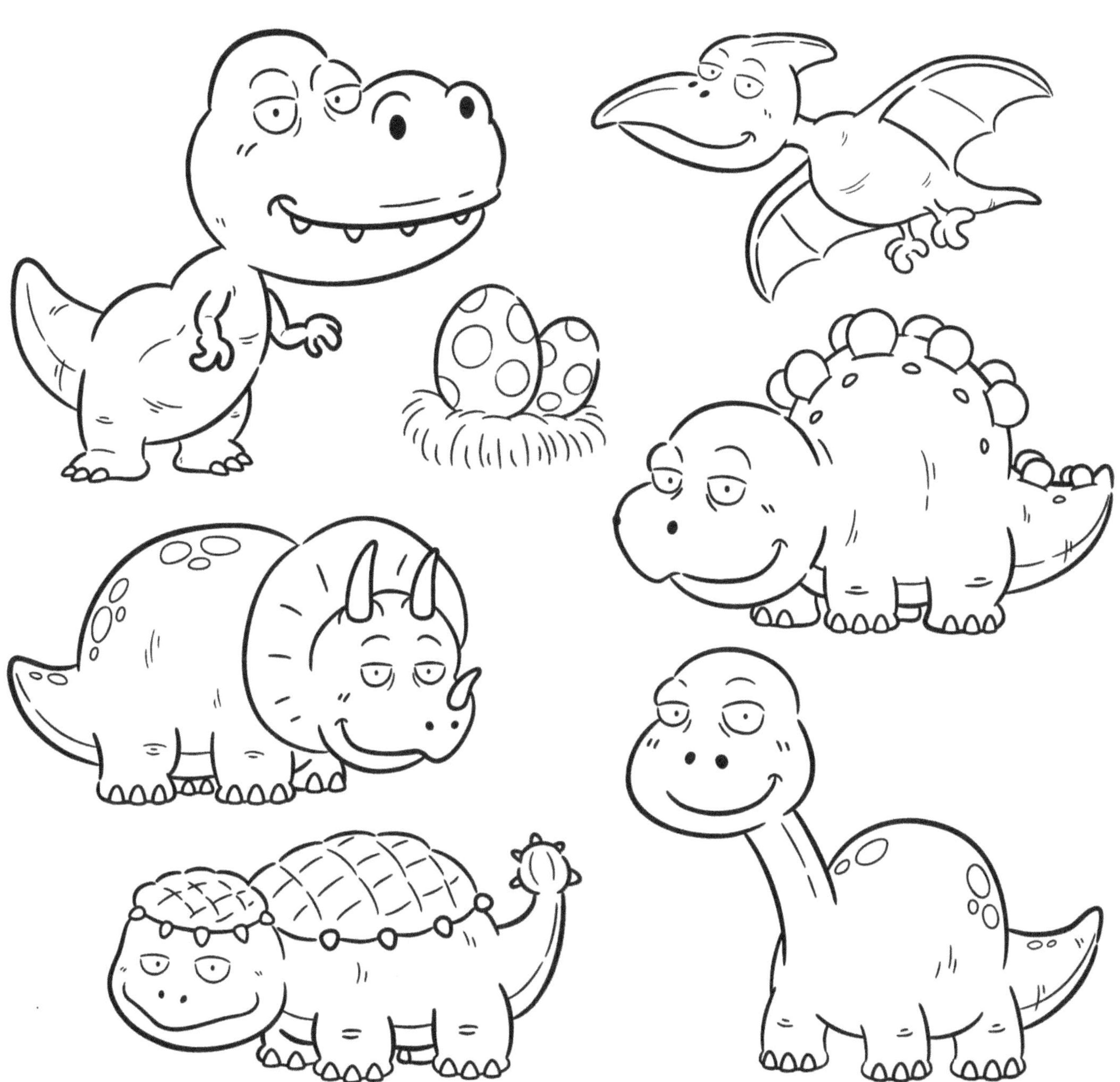

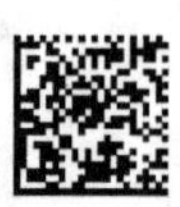
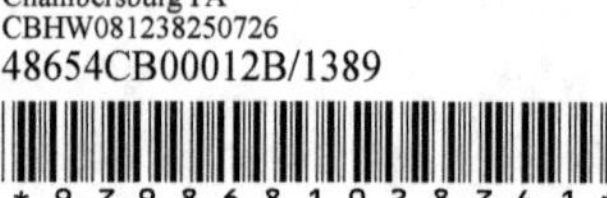
9 798681 028741